Self-Regulation and Active Problem Solving

Activities to Teach Kids How to Generalize Learned Skills to Real-Life Situations

Briana Makofske, PhD

Self-Regulation and Active Problem Solving © 2020 by Briana Makofske

Published by:

PESI Publishing & Media
PESI, Inc.
3839 White Ave.
Eau Claire, WI 54703

Cover Design: Amy Rubenzer
Editing: Jenessa Jackson, PhD
Layout: Amy Rubenzer & Bookmasters

Printed in the United States of America
ISBN: 9781683732655
All rights reserved.

pesipublishing.com

About the Author

Briana Makofske, PhD, is the co-owner of Summit Psychological Assessment & Consultation and a Licensed Psychologist and Licensed School Psychologist in the state of Colorado. She has extensive experience working with children with neurodevelopmental disorders in school settings and in private practice. She addresses children's individual needs through assessment, the development of collaborative goals and interventions, and the provision of direct and consultative services. Dr. Makofske believes that all children can acquire skills to increase their independence. The focus of her work now is collaborating with, and teaching skills to, parents and educators to support children in multiple environments.

Acknowledgments

This book would not have been possible without the support and encouragement of others. No accomplishment is mine alone, and I have several people to thank and acknowledge. First is Christie Bowers, MS CCC-SLP, who is a dear friend of mine and a valued teammate. I have had the privilege of collaborating with her to create and co-teach many of the activities in this book. Christie is a brilliant speech-language pathologist who specializes in working collaboratively with other professionals to support children and families with augmentative and alternative communication, and she is an expert at differentiation. Christie's creativity and passion for supporting children inspires me every day, and working with her has been a highlight in my career.

Jackie Walsh is a parent who pushed me to think outside of the box and is a fierce advocate for students with diverse needs. She sets incredibly high standards for herself, and she walks the walk as a parent and now as an educator. She is an amazing woman who models what dedication and perseverance look like, and I am truly thankful for how she has influenced me.

I do not know if I would have ever tackled the project of writing this book without the encouragement of my business partner, Dr. Rachel Toplis. I am so very thankful to have her as a partner because of her progressive thinking, grace, and confidence in what we do.

I would also like to thank Jenessa Jackson, PhD; Karsyn Morse; and the team at PESI for helping create a book that we can all be proud of. Having an idea is one thing, but putting it together into a meaningful product is a completely different thing, and that could not have happened without their support, feedback, and talents.

Most important, I have to thank my family, who has loved and supported me along the way. To my husband, this book is a reflection of our journey that started more than 20 years ago. I am very proud of all that we have accomplished together and know we can do anything as a team.

Table of Contents

Part 1: Introduction..1

- Why I Wrote This Book 3
- How is This Book Different?....................................... 4
- Who is This Book For? 5
- The Specific Skills Taught 6
- How to Use This Book 8
- Encouraging Parents at Home 13

Part 2: The Lesson Plans...15

- Friendship Mix... 17
- Snow Globe 27
- Pumpkin Pudding... 37
- Teacher Appreciation Cards 47
- Ornaments.. 59
- Card or Board Games 69
- Build a Vehicle 79
- Stress Ball.. 89
- Scavenger Hunt 99
- Build a Bridge 111
- Cookie Decorating.. 121
- Decorate a Door.. 135
- Peanut Butter & Jelly 147
- Back-to-Back Drawing 157
- Plan a Party 171

Appendix.. 187

- Blank Lesson Plan... 189

References 191

Introduction

As a licensed psychologist and school psychologist, I have worked extensively with children with various needs and skill sets. Much of my time has been spent working directly with children, talking with parents to learn about the concerns they have for their child, and consulting with teachers to develop interventions and strategies to support children in classrooms. Early on in my career, I developed a relationship with a family who heavily influenced how I approached my job and supported children and families. During my second year as a school psychologist, I was at one of my first individualized education program (IEP) meetings with this family when the mom sat down across from me and said, "Well, Bri, same shit, different year. What have you got?" The look on my face must have told her I needed more information because she added,

> *I know we're here to talk about Daniel's goals and progress, but he has autism, and we are now in middle school. He likes to touch girls' hair, has zero concept of money, has meltdowns over small things, and loves cars. I worry that someone will ask him for money and he will give it to them, or if someone drives by the school in a cool car, he will approach them and get in. What are you going to do, get someone to drive by in a Lamborghini and ask him if he wants candy?*

Although service providers working in educational settings are not the only ones responsible for teaching children about stranger danger and money management, my interaction with that family has always stood out in my mind and made me question what we are supposed to be doing to help children become independent.

To best support the children I worked with, I relied on research and textbooks that outlined ways to support children with various needs. I found that much of the literature focused on teaching children the skills needed to manage themselves in small, controlled settings. For example, there are books that explain how to help children with autism, attention-deficit/hyperactivity disorder (ADHD), anxiety, and several other clinical issues learn how to (1) identify their feelings, (2) identify triggers, (3) develop coping strategies, (4) discuss "what if" scenarios, and (5) come up with a plan for next time. All these books are great starting points for teaching basic skills to children (and I have my favorites), **but what I have found is that, ultimately, children only learn to apply these skills in small, controlled environments and struggle applying them in other places with other people. In other words, they are not able to generalize the learning.** My goal is always to help children become independent, and to do that, they must be able to generalize the skills they have learned to the real world.

With the Lamborghini statement in mind, I began creating small scenarios to test whether what I was teaching was sinking in and whether children could apply their skills in real-life, unpredictable situations.

WHY I WROTE THIS BOOK

As professionals, we often utilize a research-based curriculum to help children learn how to manage their emotions and problem solve a variety of situations. We know that in structured environments, many children are able to demonstrate self-regulation and coping skills by talking through possible what-if scenarios that describe what they "should" do "if" something happens. We then create beautiful classroom supports, facilitate the transition into the classroom by coaching the teacher on the skills we have practiced, and prepare children to go to the classroom with the hope that the skills they have learned will be generalized.

However, once children enter the classroom, the unpredictable happens. Someone may have taken their chair, they cannot find their pencil, they did not like the activity, a peer made a sarcastic remark, they were excited to share their thoughts and did not get called on, or the teacher may have changed the routine of the day—the list goes on and on. On any given day, outside of small-group environments, children encounter multiple, unpredictable stressors, which require flexibility and the ability to think on their feet. Although we spend a lot of time on the front end, we often end up problem solving and debriefing with children *after* they have become dysregulated or upset.

Although most books provide a strong foundation for teaching kids the skills needed to manage themselves, they do not necessarily tell us what to do to help children generalize those skills across a variety of situations. Simply put, there is a gap between what we teach children in small, structured group settings and what we expect them to do in classrooms or other environments, mostly because active problem solving is always a requirement. **Learning self-regulation skills without the ability to problem solve or generalize these skills does not lead to independence.** Therefore, I decided to write this book to provide professionals with a variety of creative ways that they can challenge children to apply active problem-solving and self-regulation skills in more challenging environments that are more unpredictable and reflect real-life scenarios.

HOW IS THIS BOOK DIFFERENT?

If you have purchased this book, then you are looking to help the students you support bridge the gap between small-group success and success in the classroom or other environments. **Unlike most books that teach specific, individual skills in a controlled environment, this book teaches practitioners how to help children generalize the skills they have learned and apply them to a variety of real-life situations.** To do so, the activities in this book ask children to implement the skills they have learned *while* they are dysregulated, during a stressful situation, or when active problem solving is required. When children can successfully apply these strategies while they are dysregulated, they will be more likely to generalize those skills to other settings—and when individuals are able to generalize skills in multiple environments, they become more independent.

The activities in this book present clients with opportunities to practice their problem-solving skills in a familiar environment to promote success. Activities are intended to be reviewed, practiced, and repeated. Small, reasonable challenges are incrementally added as students become better and better at problem solving so that they gain confidence and learn the tools needed to problem solve outside of the small-group environment. When students are able to practice applying coping strategies and other self-regulation techniques successfully in a small group while feeling overwhelmed, frustrated, or upset, they will be more likely to generalize those skills in other environments.

By introducing some common stressors that students will likely encounter, the activities in this book will also allow you to observe how individuals respond when they become overwhelmed. Some students shut down, others complain, and, at times, some have a meltdown. When this happens, you'll learn how to provide direct feedback **in the moment** that will help them move forward. In the end, you will help them learn how to overcome something stressful, gain confidence, generalize their skills, and set them up for success in other environments.

The situations we encounter in real life are never exactly the same, so learning to actively problem solve is an essential life skill. Indeed, we cannot possibly teach or plan for every single scenario our clients will experience or come across. What we can do is require them to apply the skills we have taught them in a safe environment that gradually becomes more challenging. It is no different than when we learned how to drive a car. Think for a minute about how most of us learned to drive. We sat in a large, empty parking lot; put the keys in the ignition; pressed the break; checked our blind spots; turned the car on; put the car into gear; placed our hands at 10:00 and 2:00; and slowly pressed the gas. After mastering a large, empty parking lot, we gained some confidence, and our parents made us drive on the side roads in the neighborhood. Eventually, our parents gave us permission to drive to the grocery store and back.

Experience on the road taught us the most about driving, and after a while, things became second nature; we no longer needed one of our parents riding in the front seat directing or prompting us. Over time, through repetition and gradual increases of stress, we learned how to adapt to high-stress situations while driving with other people on the road and generalized our skills so that we could safely maneuver high-traffic areas and safely get to our destination. What we did *not* do is master driving in a large, empty parking lot, get onto the interstate, and then attempt to maneuver downtown traffic during rush hour. The same goes for teaching children emotion regulation, planning, problem solving, and other related skills: Before we send children into a classroom or other unpredictable settings to apply the skills they have learned, we need to first create scenarios and situations that require active problem solving so that they can *practice* applying these strategies while feeling frustrated, overwhelmed, or dysregulated. With this approach, I have seen children gain confidence and the ability to be flexible—which, in turn, has allowed them to access their environment and build meaningful relationships.

WHO IS THIS BOOK FOR?

This book has been written with the special service provider in mind. It is intended for providers who work in school settings and typically teach students specific skills outside of the general education classroom. This includes special education teachers, school psychologists, social workers, speech and language pathologists, occupational therapists, counselors, and behavior interventionists. **This book is for you if you do the following:**

- Teach children specific skills outside of the classroom
- Use specific curricula to expand students' skill sets
- Consult with parents and professionals as to how they can support children outside of a small-group setting
- Recognize a disconnect between what students can do in a small-group setting versus the general classroom
- Want to address multiple skills sets in one setting
- Want to enable children to apply their skills outside of a small, controlled environment

- Need language to communicate with parents that describes how students' needs are being met
- Want fun and easy-to-implement activities that teach independence skills
- Want activities that give you the most "bang for your buck"
- Want activities that teach skills needed in academic environments
- Want activities that align easily with IEP goals

I have written this book to encourage special service providers to expand beyond the mind-set of "teaching specific skills" curriculum and, instead, to intentionally incorporate challenges into the controlled environment so that students can practice applying the skills they have learned while they are in a state of dysregulation. The ideas and activities in this book are not targeted for any one particular type of disorder and can be useful for all children with all types of challenges. Children who benefit from the activities in this book include those who have difficulty interacting with their peers, following directions, controlling their impulses, advocating for their needs, taking turns, staying on task, and adjusting to changes in their environment. You may find the activities in this book the most helpful for children diagnosed with the following:

- Autism spectrum disorder
- ADHD
- Specific learning disorder
- Anxiety disorders
- Communication disorders
- Adjustment disorders

THE SPECIFIC SKILLS TAUGHT

Typically, the types of behaviors that are difficult for students to generalize from the classroom to more uncontrolled settings include frustration tolerance, self-regulation, cognitive flexibility, self-awareness, self-advocacy, and active problem solving. As service providers, our role is to support their skill deficits. Not all skills can be learned and mastered; some children need to learn strategies to make them successful in applying these skills, which is what *we* teach. We need to teach them if, when, and how to apply these skills—and to then *practice* doing so in unpredictable and stressful environments.

The activities outlined in this book will provide you with opportunities to tackle multiple skill deficits for several individuals at the same time. Each activity includes a list of targeted skills that we want to see students demonstrate—*not* behaviors that we want to see eliminated. Outlining the skills we want to see students demonstrate helps us clearly communicate to others what we are tackling during sessions with students. The following chart provides a summary of the activities in this book, as well as the accompanying skills that each activity targets. For any of these activities to be successful, you must first have the following:

- A trusting, positive relationship with the student
- Directly taught specific self-regulation strategies

- An understanding of individual skill deficits and IEP goals
- Knowledge of challenges that students are facing in the classroom
- Opportunity for small-group instruction involving approximately 1 to 8 students
- Flexibility
- An understanding that not all activities will go smoothly
- An instructor who can become an active participant, not just a facilitator

Skill Deficit \ Activity	Friendship Mix	Snow Globe	Pumpkin Pudding	Teacher Appreciation Cards	Ornaments	Card or Board Games	Build a Vehicle	Stress Ball	Scavenger Hunt	Build a Bridge	Cookie Decorating	Decorate a Door	Peanut Butter & Jelly	Back-to-Back Drawing	Plan a Party
Collaboration			•	•		•	•			•	•	•			•
Cooperation	•	•	•	•	•	•	•	•	•	•	•	•	•	•	•
Emotion Regulation		•		•		•	•	•		•	•	•	•	•	•
Expressive Language				•		•			•	•	•	•	•	•	
Flexibility/Shifting	•	•		•	•	•	•	•	•	•	•	•	•		•
Following Directions		•	•	•	•	•	•	•	•	•	•	•	•	•	•
Frustration Tolerance	•	•	•	•	•	•	•	•	•	•	•	•	•	•	•
Impulsivity	•	•	•	•	•	•	•	•	•	•	•	•	•	•	•
Initiation	•		•	•	•	•	•		•	•	•	•	•	•	•
Life Skills	•	•	•		•	•			•	•	•	•	•		•
Listening	•	•	•		•	•			•	•	•			•	•
Locus of Control	•					•	•			•	•	•	•		•
Organization		•	•	•	•		•	•		•	•	•		•	•
Planning	•	•	•	•	•	•	•	•		•	•	•	•	•	•
Problem Solving	•	•	•	•	•	•	•	•	•	•	•	•	•	•	•
Recognizing Nonverbal Cues	•					•	•		•			•	•		•
Self-Advocacy	•	•	•	•	•	•	•	•	•	•	•	•	•	•	•
Self-Regulation/Self-Monitoring	•	•				•	•	•		•	•	•	•	•	•
Sequencing		•	•	•	•	•			•	•	•	•	•	•	•
Shared Attention	•	•	•		•	•	•	•	•	•	•	•	•	•	•
Taking Turns	•	•	•	•	•	•	•	•	•	•	•			•	•
Theory of Mind		•	•			•			•						•
Working Memory			•			•									

The ultimate goal for each activity is for students to demonstrate these skills *independently*. That means without prompts and in the moment. Often, students do need support and prompts, and that is expected when they require small-group instruction. However, presenting them with situations where they have to try it on their own is important, or you will never know if they can do it independently.

Given that the ultimate goal is for students to demonstrate independence, when you are writing IEP or performance goals related to skill acquisition, you want to consider the student's level of independence with the task rather than the number of times they demonstrates a specific skill. For example, "Student will cross the street *independently* when getting on and off the school bus by stopping at the appropriate intersection, looking both ways, and walking to the other side," as opposed to "Student will successfully cross the street four out of five times when getting on and off the school bus by stopping at the appropriate intersection, looking both ways, and walking to the other side." Because crossing the street four out of five times is not acceptable due to obvious safety concerns, we offer and scaffold support until we are confident the student can do the behavior 100% of the time.

Another real-life example is when potty-training children. When we start, we go in the bathroom with the child and guide him or her through the entire process. Over time, we offer less guidance, knowing that the ultimate goal is for the child to be 100% independent. I do not plan to go to college with my child and stand outside of the bathroom with a jellybean. I see problem solving and self-regulation as important life skills that should not happen only sometimes. Therefore, when creating goals for clients, I encourage you to think about whether the child needs to eventually do the skill independently and that establishing independence needs to happen before tracking frequency.

HOW TO USE THIS BOOK

To successfully implement the activities outlined in this book, keep the following eight points in mind:

1. **Read the lesson plan before you begin.**

    Familiarize yourself with the activity so that you are better able to focus on addressing student skill development. Each lesson plan has notes for you to consider so you are better prepared. The "preparation" section lists what you need to have completed before students arrive.

2. **Provide students with necessary accommodations and support.**

    Always have steps outlined so that students can see and refer to them. **Always** post expectations for appropriate behavior so that students can see them and so you can refer to them frequently. Many people have very different opinions on what "appropriate" behaviors look like. What does "appropriate" mean and look like in your group? Have a clear definition and communicate it to the students. **Always** preteach vocabulary required for the students to participate in the activity and post it in the room if necessary. This reduces some language and vocabulary demands that can interfere with the objectives of the activities.

3. **Model the activities first.**

    The amount of modeling you provide throughout the session is dependent on age and skill level. You can model each step or provide an example of a final product so students can see what they are working toward. Modeling can be done by an adult or another student. If you choose to use another student, be sure to prepare them before the group comes.

4. **Be an active participant.**

    By actively participating, you are better able to insert challenges throughout the activity. When you are involved in the activity, students are less likely to look to you for answers or guidance before attempting something. At the same time, you can jump in to suggest a strategy when students become overwhelmed or when their threshold is being met.

5. **Do not let avoidance get in the way.**

    When students perceive a task as being difficult, they will do what they can to avoid doing the task. Do not allow students to completely avoid the task because it is hard or makes them uncomfortable. **Integrating reasonable challenges forces students to problem solve in the moment and advocate for their needs.** Find a way for students to successfully get through the task, even if it means that they contribute very little that day. The point is that the student gets through a difficult task successfully so you can continue to build skills. When an activity does not go smoothly, it also serves as a learning opportunity for you. You can repeat the activity and set different expectations or tweak the steps to help the students practice different skills and try new things.

6. **Let students fail.**

    Activities do not have to be completed smoothly or perfectly. Mistakes and imperfections are what provide the best learning opportunities that reflect real life. You are highly encouraged to *not* problem solve for the students. When doing these activities, appear as though you have never done the activity before. Make comments or ask questions such as the following:

    "Where would I find something like that?"

    "I wonder what we can do to figure this out?"

    "What do other kids do when this happens?"

    "When I am not sure what to do, I will ask someone."

    "I think I might need to look that up."

    Take notes on your lesson plan sheet with what was successful and what was challenging, and plan accordingly the next time to make the experience more successful. You can either repeat an activity and see how students adjust their behaviors and problem-solving approaches or attempt a different type of activity with additional supports that meet students at their level.

7. **Give feedback in the moment.**

    The activities in this book facilitate opportunities in which students can become frustrated and overwhelmed, and you can catch early signs of dysregulation and provide feedback in the moment. Gently highlighting the moment that students start to become frustrated or emotional—and reflecting what you see—will help them become more aware of what they are feeling, how they are behaving, and how they are being perceived by others. It provides them an opportunity to recognize what is happening and attempt a strategy to self-regulate, either on their own or with the help of an adult. Once they have attempted a strategy, you can then provide them with the next steps so they can move past the stressful experience and ultimately complete the task. The following is an example of how you can reflect to students to provide them with feedback in the moment:

"You seem [*feeling*]."

"I can tell because you are [*observed behavior*]."

"Now will be a good time to [*strategy*]."

"Then, we can talk about what to do next [*plan*]."

8. Provide necessary accommodations.

Any accommodation that a teacher is required to implement in the classroom should be implemented in the context of the small-group activity so that students know what it looks and feels like. When you provide accommodations for students in small-group formats, you are better able to communicate to the classroom teacher what you have worked on, what worked in your group, and help the teacher tweak or adjust how accommodations function in their individual classrooms. The following are some examples of accommodations:

- Provide examples of final products.
- Provide a predictable sequence to an activity.
- Define each student's role in group activities.
- Define steps within a task.
- Provide wait time for responses to questions in class.
- Secure students' attention before communicating.
- Provide opportunities for students to initiate interactions.
- Clearly define the beginning and end of an activity.
- Provide access to word processing or other writing accommodations.
- Let students know when to expect their turn.
- Pair all written materials with visuals.
- Clearly post classroom and school expectations.
- Break longer tasks into short, manageable steps.

Activity and Lesson Plan Structure

This book contains 15 different activities that cover at least 30 sessions, all of which are highly engaging and follow the exact same structure and process. Although the activities in this book represent "games" for students to play, the activities are never as much fun as students initially think they will be. This is because I have established standard expectations that when students come to group, they are expected to (1) problem solve, (2) work together and cooperate, (3) manage their emotions, and (4) advocate for themselves. The goal for each session is to create a safe environment that facilitates active problem solving when students become upset or dysregulated rather than solely practicing when they are in a calm state.

Some activities in this book take longer to complete, and that is okay because the point is to address skill deficits, not to complete the task perfectly. Although I have organized the activities from easiest to most difficult, the activities do not need to be presented sequentially and can be completed throughout the school year in conjunction with other curricula. In addition, all the activities can be completed more than once, or as often as necessary, so students have more opportunities to practice and so you can see how they adjust their behaviors to make the activity go more smoothly. A brief description of the lesson plan and activity structure is as follows:

1. **Summary:** Each activity begins with a brief description of what will be presented to students and what the task involves.

2. **Objectives/Goals:** The overarching targets and objectives for each activity are spelled out, but you can include additional IEP goals on the lesson plan sheet as well. This can serve as documentation for how you address student needs.

3. **Skills Supported:** Each activity lists the required skills to be successful with the task at hand. The specific skills covered in each activity are also outlined in the table on page 7.

4. **Number of Students:** All the activities require more than one participant and have a maximum suggested number of students for the activity to run smoothly. The more students you have, the more complicated the activity is and the more problem solving is required. If you are working with one child at a time, then you will serve as the other participant who is problem solving with the child. When this is the case, provide suggestions as though you are a same-age peer; do not provide solutions.

5. **Materials:** All required materials are listed on the first page of each activity. Some activities require the purchase of materials, but you may already have several of these items lying around your home or office. Writing out or displaying the materials needed for each activity is important, as this gives students a visual for what they are going to be doing, which allows them to come up with a plan before starting.

6. **Preparation:** Each activity lists a variety of tasks to complete and issues to consider before beginning the activity.

7. **Introduction:** A description of the activity is provided, with accompanying expectations and directions so that students know what they will be attempting.

8. **Expectations:** The specific expectations for each activity are laid out. **Clearly defined expectations are the most important part of each activity**. Having expectations clearly posted where all students can see them and that you go through each one together prior to beginning the activity is suggested. When expectations are clearly outlined and posted, students are less likely to argue when redirected and can be redirected more easily. You are encouraged to add any behaviors you have been teaching throughout the school year to the list of expectations.

9. **Steps:** Each activity lists the specific steps required to complete the task. When presenting the lesson to students, simplify the steps.

10. **Challenges to Incorporate:** Quick and easy ideas for challenges that can be presented for each activity are outlined for you. Challenges are all things that you intentionally do to make activities more difficult and are noted with either a +/− symbol. The + symbol indicates the addition of a stressor, something you insert to make the task more difficult. You can control how many stressors you add to the task, which is how you can scaffold and differentiate each task based on what the students can handle or what they need to learn. The − symbol is the removal of something that students expect to be part of the task. Removing things from the task encourages students to problem solve and advocate for themselves. Either way, knowing what types of situations cause your students to become overwhelmed, you can mix and match adding stressors or removing expected components with the ultimate goal of sabotaging the activity so that students are required to problem solve and self-regulate.

11. **Differentiation for Age or Skill Level:** Suggestions as to how you can differentiate the task based on age or skill level are provided for each activity. For example, if problem solving is the goal, then you can provide less instruction. If self-regulation is the goal, then you can add more unexpected challenges. The age and skill levels in this book are defined as follows:

    - Beginner: Younger students or students at a lower skill level who require adult support
    - Intermediate: Middle school-age students or students who rely on prompts
    - Advanced: Older students and high-functioning students

12. **Reflection:** Each activity includes a description of how to best reflect on and debrief following the activity. Facilitating a discussion after the activity helps students talk about what they felt proud of and what they could have done differently, which helps them problem solve for next time.

13. **Follow-Up:** Suggestions for additional activities that can be presented at the next session to support student growth are provided with each activity.

14. **Generalization to the Classroom:** A brief explanation is provided to describe how the activity reflects or simulates classroom activities.

15. **Instructor Notes and Thoughts:** Following each activity, blank spaces are provided where you can record any observations or overall impressions about how the activity went, including what you might to do differently next time or what you might keep the same.

16. **Lesson Plan:** Each activity includes an accompanying lesson plan outline, which is intended to serve as simple documentation for what you did on a particular day, how the students performed, how they progressed toward their goals, and what you can do next time. The lesson plan can be used as a form of data collection and as observation notes for you as the instructor. The lesson plan outline also supports how you will present the activity to students and model organization and planning. An example lesson plan is attached to each activity, along with a blank lesson plan sheet at the end of this book (see the Appendix).

17. **Reflection Sheets:** For each activity, reflection sheets are included with follow-up questions that provide students an opportunity to reinforce what they have

learned and practice their writing skills. Reflection sheets do not always need to be used, but they can help guide discussion for the problem-solving process.

18. **Case Example:** Each activity concludes with a case example, which describes some of the direct experiences I have had with students. Each example highlights some of the different challenges students have faced and how I supported them in the context of the activities. The case examples also illustrate how the desirability of the activities increases the likelihood that students will work through some of their struggles and even see some humor in the tasks. My experiences with students have helped me grow and learn to adapt the activities so that I can continue to provide them with experiences that help them learn. Many of the case examples reference Christie Bowers, a speech-language pathologist with whom I was able to often collaborate. Reading through some of my experiences might jump-start your thinking and give you some confidence to dive in.

As you become comfortable with the process, you will be able to apply the outline and strategies to any activity you present in a small group. You can get very creative and will be surprised at what you come up with and what students can accomplish.

ENCOURAGING PARENTS AT HOME

In addition to the activities and lesson plans provided in this book, the best way to ensure that children generalize the skills they have learned with you is to have them practice these skills at home as well. Collaborating with families to develop consistent expectations and language use will support the child's development of independence. By utilizing the same approach to the activities in this book, you can encourage parents to incorporate challenges at home that will require their child to problem solve.

Share with parents that their job is to add a small challenge to an activity that they typically take care of for their child. Parents tend to pick up a lot of slack for their children due to time constraints, frustration levels, and a need for things to go smoothly (when they can ☺). Talking with parents about this approach to problem solving and independence will provide them with an opportunity to think about ways they can increase their child's independence at home. Ideally, the skills and behaviors you are working on in the therapeutic setting are similar to those parents are working on at home. Collaborate with parents to help them choose one to three things that their child can become more independent with at home, and help them set up a simple system to do it successfully. This includes having pictures and checklists, as well as making sure that parents model for their child how to do an activity the first time. The following are some things parents can require their child to do independently:

- Putting clothes away
- Packing their backpack
- Cleaning their bedroom
- Packing their lunch
- Taking out the trash (or completing other chores) without multiple reminders

Once parents begin to increase their child's independence with daily tasks, they can then begin to add in small challenges. Ultimately, you want to encourage parents to do the same thing you are doing: incorporate small challenges that require children to problem solve *independently.* When doing so, parents need to think about when it will be appropriate to incorporate these challenges at home. For example, trying to tackle packing a backpack in the morning when the family is rushing out the door is probably not a good idea. However, if they have some time on a Saturday, parents can plan ahead—with the understanding that the activity may not go smoothly and that it will take time out of their day—and accomplish a challenging task with their child. Any craft or family game can be an opportunity for parents to practice the skills you are teaching in your setting. The following are some examples of challenges that parents can incorporate:

- Make cupcakes but do not have all the materials readily available
- Set the table with only knives
- Play a game with the family and go out of turn
- Misplace the child's shoes

At the end of the day, children's development and success are dependent on their environment and the teaching and support provided by the adults in their lives. When we all work together and have similar expectations and follow-through, we increase the likelihood of success. A parent is a child's first and most influential teacher, and sometimes, we have opportunities to add tools to their toolbox that will help them continue to support their child's growth and development. The activities in this book and the philosophy behind them are tools we can all use to help children make gains toward becoming independent.

Part 2:
The Lesson Plans

SUMMARY

The group will be making a fun snack, and students will be required to interact with one another to meet their needs. This very simple activity can be done with all age groups with various needs. This fun beginning activity teaches students what to expect for future sessions.

OBJECTIVE/GOALS

- Students will interact with other people to get their needs met appropriately.
- Students will recognize when it is their turn to interject or make a request.
- Students will share resources with others.

SKILLS SUPPORTED

- Cooperation
- Flexibility
- Frustration Tolerance
- Impulsivity
- Initiation
- Life Skills
- Listening
- Locus of Control
- Planning
- Problem Solving
- Recognizing Nonverbal Cues
- Self-Advocacy
- Self-Regulation
- Shared Attention
- Taking Turns

NUMBER OF STUDENTS

- 1–6

MATERIALS

- Any food kids like to mix (e.g., cereal, dry snacks, chocolate, candy, marshmallows)
- Cups
- Napkins
- Spoons

PREPARATION

__ Check for allergies.

__ Purchase snack items.

__ Make an example of a mix to show students.

__ Create visual with expectations.

__ Create visual with outlined steps.

INTRODUCTION

Students will be making a snack called "friendship mix" using whatever ingredients from the table they choose to add to their cup. Each student will be responsible for holding one ingredient, and that student will be in charge of passing out the ingredient whenever another student asks for some. Ingredients will not be passed around the table; if a student wants a particular ingredient (e.g., marshmallows), then he or she must ask for it.

Ask students to look at all the ingredients to get an idea of what they would like to put in their cup. Students must incorporate at least three ingredients and wait until everyone is done before they eat their snack. Once you have outlined the expectations, the students should be fairly independent when creating their mix. However, they may need reminders to wait their turn or to ask politely.

EXPECTATIONS

Before you begin, review the expectations for the group and emphasize any behaviors you want to see during the session:

- Wash your hands first.
- Wait your turn.
- Ask politely.
- You must include at least three ingredients.
- Share.
- _____
- _____

STEPS

1. Show students your mix as a model for what they are going to make.
2. Require students to wash their hands.
3. Give each student one ingredient to hold and be in charge of. **Dispersing the ingredients among students forces them to interact with one another.** It also tests whether they are able to recognize and interpret nonverbal cues from others as to when they can interject or ask for something. In contrast, if you place ingredients in the middle of the table, then students can continue to work by themselves and never have to ask for what they need.

4. Discuss what it means to be in charge of the ingredient: The student is supposed to hand it out to others who request some of it (e.g., marshmallows). Some students may argue that they do not want the ingredient you have chosen for them and that they prefer their favorite. **This is the first opportunity for you to support flexibility and self-advocacy.**

5. Encourage students to get a cup and look around the table for which ingredients they want to add to their mix. **This is a chance for you to see if they preplan or look to see what other people have.**

6. Share with students that they can only get an ingredient for their cup if they wait their turn and ask another student for the ingredient they want in an *appropriate* manner.

7. Discuss what "appropriate" means and what it looks like. Being appropriate requires students to look around to see what other people are doing and to be aware of how they ask for things. Often, students will try to reach across the table or will be overly demanding. Model and practice appropriate behaviors before students start.

8. Make the mix, and instruct students to wait until everyone is finished before they eat. This is the first activity where you can observe and take notes about what types of challenges you need to incorporate to provide opportunities for each student to practice the learned skills.

9. Eat the snack together, and reflect on how the activity went.

CHALLENGES TO INCORPORATE

− Do not give the desired ingredient; be stubborn.

− Do not have cups available on the table.

+ Grab ingredients from a student without asking.

+ Whine about what you want.

+ Break a rule or expectation (e.g., start eating before everyone is finished).

DIFFERENTIATION FOR AGE OR SKILL LEVEL

- **Beginner:** Be sure to have the steps *explicitly* outlined somewhere visible; this is not an activity that should require problem solving. Establish an order for students to follow when it comes to taking turns so that they are more successful in doing so. Challenges should be simple (e.g., do not place spoons or cups out on the table, but have them somewhere close—as if you forgot them in the bag).

- **Intermediate:** Be an active participant and insert challenges by breaking rules. Be a difficult peer.

- **Advanced:** Do not interject at all and see how the activity moves forward. Doing so is a good opportunity to establish a baseline for how independent the group is with minimal instruction and how the students interact without adult prompting. If students complete the activity silently, then you know that you need to provide more support next time to facilitate more interaction.

REFLECTION

Because this activity is simple, the reflection centers on what types of things made the activity hard and how each student managed his or her feelings.

FOLLOW-UP

You can play a card game, such as UNO®, Go Fish, or, for older students, Spades, for your next session to implement the skills you practiced during this session. Reiterate how students take turns and how they look around the table to see what other students are doing. If this was a challenging activity, repeat it again in two weeks and see if students make any adjustments to their behaviors as they will have had experience doing the activity and will know what to expect. Other activities that require similar skills include the following:

- Card or Board Games
- Snow Globe
- Build a Vehicle

GENERALIZATION TO THE CLASSROOM

This activity simulates classroom activities in which students have to work with others to create a product, as often occurs in the context of physical education class or science lab.

INSTRUCTOR NOTES AND THOUGHTS

_____
_____
_____
_____
_____
_____

LESSON PLAN EXAMPLE: Friendship Mix

Date: _____06/12_____

Activity: _____Friendship Mix_____

Students:

_____Jake_____ _____Logan_____

_____Sara_____ _____Gabe_____

_____Sasha_____ _____

Materials:

- ☐ Cereal
- ☐ Dry snack
- ☐ Chocolate
- ☐ Candy
- ☐ Marshmallows
- ☐ Cups
- ☐ Napkins
- ☐ Spoons

Expectations:

- Wash your hands first.
- Wait your turn.
- Ask for ingredients from your peers politely.
- Share.
- Wait until everyone is finished making their mix before eating.
- You must include at least three ingredients.

Steps to Complete:

1. Wash your hands first.
2. Get out materials.
3. Decide what you want in your mix (at least three ingredients).
4. Ask others for the ingredients you want.
5. Wait until everyone is finished.
6. Eat.

Successes:
- Logan was very patient and made sure everyone was finished before beginning. He took on a leadership role.
- Most students were engaged and excited to try the activity.

Challenges:
- Sara reached across table and became frustrated when redirected to ask politely (e.g., yelled, "I hate this!").
- Jake refused to share the candy and only put them in his cup. He ignored other students.

Next Time:
- Review expectations more thoroughly before beginning the activity.
- Model the activity with another adult before starting.
- Give Jake a job to start the activity so he is engaged from the beginning (e.g., pass out materials, etc.).

STUDENT REFLECTION: Friendship Mix

Date: _____

Activity: _____

Who was here today?

_____   _____

_____   _____

_____   _____

What did you do today?

Today we _____

_____

_____

_____

How did it make you feel?

- ☐ Satisfied
- ☐ Confident
- ☐ Happy
- ☐ Frustrated
- ☐ Irritated
- ☐ Anxious
- ☐ Bored
- ☐ Sad
- ☐ Shy
- ☐ _____
- ☐ _____
- ☐ _____

What did you do well today?

Today I was able to _____

_____

_____

_____

What was the hardest part of the activity?

The hardest part of the activity today was _____

_____

_____

_____

What will you do differently next time?

Next time, I will _____

_____

_____

_____

What can you do in class when things do not go your way?

In class, I can _____

_____

_____

_____

When do you have to do something like this in class?

In class, I have to take turns and share when we _____

_____

_____

_____

# Friendship Mix

Chris, a second-grade student diagnosed with oppositional defiant disorder, had difficulty following directions in the classroom and frequently argued with his peers. When he perceived a task as difficult and was prompted by an adult, he would refuse to participate, yell at others, call them names, and engage in a power struggle for hours. Chris's outbursts often led to him missing class activities, and other children did not want to play with him.

I worked with Chris individually each week to identify the triggers for his emotional outbursts and to try new strategies for managing his emotions and behaviors to stay engaged with a task. When I felt he was ready, I talked with him about inviting three other students to join our session to make a snack together. He was very eager to invite some classmates, and I asked the teacher which students would be a good fit before arranging for them to join us. I also shared with Chris that although we would be making a snack, the activity was not just intended to be fun; we would still have to work on problem solving and interacting with others appropriately as well.

When the students arrived, I had all the expectations written out on a whiteboard with the activity title and steps outlined. We reviewed all the expectations and talked about how to ask a peer for an ingredient nicely. I reiterated that we had plenty of time to complete the snack and eat it together. I then pulled out all my ingredients (e.g., marshmallows, pretzels, Skittles®, M&M®s, and Cheerios®) and placed napkins on the table. Chris immediately yelled out, "Skittles are not in trail mix!" I responded by stating that it was called friendship mix and that each of us could pick whichever three ingredients we wanted. I also redirected him to the expectations, to which he replied, "Okay, but I'm not putting Skittles in mine." I handed each student one ingredient and Chris quietly complained, "I want the marshmallows," as I handed him the pretzels. He looked at the student with the marshmallows and asked, "Can I have some of those?" Mission accomplished!

As the students began asking for ingredients, they looked around the table and asked me, "What are we supposed to put our food in?" I shrugged and said I was not sure. They then proceeded to unfold their napkins and put ingredients on the napkins. I told them that the napkins were for cleanup, and they said they had nowhere to put their mix. I asked what they thought they needed, and they suggested a cup or bowl. When I asked where they could get those, Chris yelled, "In the teacher's lounge!" They all agreed that was a good idea, but I had to stop them and encourage them to ask me for what they needed. Finally, one student asked, "Do you know where we can get some cups?" I then pulled them out from under the table and asked Chris to hand each person a cup. The students then politely created their mix, and Chris offered to pour pretzels in each person's cup. When one student said, "No, thank you," Chris paused and changed his approach to "Does anyone want pretzels?"

In the end, most of the students ended up filling their cup with mostly Skittles, M&Ms, and marshmallows (I should have anticipated that a little better), and we talked about our favorite movies. After that activity, I was able to incorporate Chris into some small-group activities for the remainder of the school year, and he continuously improved how he approached and listened to others in small group. We still had some work to do in the classroom.

Snow Globe

SUMMARY

The group will be making a snow globe to give as a gift for someone. This activity requires students to follow a sequence of directions and to think about what another person may like (e.g., as a gift recipient). It is a great activity that can be done before a holiday.

OBJECTIVE/GOALS

- Students will follow a sequence of directions successfully.
- Students will consider others' viewpoints/preferences when making a decision.
- Students will share resources with others.

SKILLS SUPPORTED

- Cooperation
- Emotion Regulation
- Flexibility
- Following Directions
- Frustration Tolerance
- Impulsivity
- Life Skills
- Listening
- Organization
- Planning
- Problem Solving
- Self-Advocacy
- Self-Regulation
- Sequencing
- Shared Attention
- Taking Turns
- Theory of Mind

NUMBER OF STUDENTS

- 1–5

MATERIALS

- Water
- Small Mason jars (1 per person)
- Small figurines
- Glitter (2–3 colors)
- Pure glycerin
- Waterproof craft glue
- Spoons
- Funnel

PREPARATION

__ Purchase the items.

__ Make a model/final product to show students.

__ Create visual with expectations.

__ Create visual with outlined steps.

INTRODUCTION

Students will be making a snow globe as a gift for someone. They will get to choose a small jar and a figurine to put into it. Students need to decide who they would like to give their snow globe to and to consider what that person likes before choosing the figurine to put into the jar. Once the snow globe has been made, students will leave it with you until the end of the day so that it has time to dry.

EXPECTATIONS

Before you begin, review the expectations for the group and emphasize any behaviors you want to see during the session:

- Wash your hands first.
- Follow directions in order.
- Check to see that all materials are available before starting.
- Help each other if someone gets stuck.
- Share.
- Be patient.
- Ask politely.
- _____
- _____

STEPS

1. Require students to wash their hands first.
2. Show them your snow globe so that they know what they are working toward.
3. Place all materials in the middle of the table.
4. Ask students to think about who they want to give the snow globe to and to think about what that person likes (e.g., colors, figurines). Then, ask students to write down the name of the intended gift recipient.
5. Instruct students to choose a Mason jar.
6. Take the lid off the jar and turn it over.
7. Instruct students to choose a figurine. **This will be the first opportunity to highlight that they are choosing something they think someone else will like, *not* what they like.** You may have to pause and guide a discussion about how students pay attention to what other people like, including what behaviors or cues serve as a signal that they are probably right.

8. Place the figurine on the Mason jar lid and see if it fits. Then, place the jar over the figurine to see that the jar fits over the whole thing. **Some figurines may be too large, and this forces students to be flexible. It provides an opportunity to test their ability to self-regulate when things do not go as expected or desired.**

9. When everything fits, glue the figurine to the inside of the lid and set it aside.

10. Allow students to choose a color of glitter and to pour some glitter into the bottom of the Mason jar. Start with a small amount (about a tablespoon) and gradually add more as desired. Too much glitter can make it difficult to see the figurine and ruin the effect of the snow globe. Students will not know how it looks until they add water and try to shake it.

11. Pour water into the jar, but do not fill it to the top. If a student added too much glitter in the previous step, decide whether you will let them start over. **This is an opportunity to discuss following directions before beginning and/or thinking before you act.**

12. Put the figurine in the jar to see if there is enough water or if it overflows. Do not close the lid or turn the jar over at this time.

13. Add two to five drops of glycerin to the glitter-and-water mixture so that the glitter falls slowly.

14. Once the figurine is dry, apply glue to the rim of the lid and the threads of the jar, and screw the lid onto the jar.

15. Turn the jar over and allow it to dry.

16. Students will leave their snow globes with you until the end of the day. **This is an opportunity to discuss how they can remind themselves to pick something up at a later time.** They may need support in coming up with an effective strategy, depending on their age and skill level. Some students will need a note sent to class, or others may need a sticky note placed in their planner.

CHALLENGES TO INCORPORATE

– Skip a step in the directions (e.g., do not say when to add glitter).

– Do not have all the necessary materials out.

+ Provide figurines that are too large.

+ Be adamant that you will get the figurine you want (this highlights how students respond to others who are pushy and provides you with an opportunity to help them advocate for themselves).

DIFFERENTIATION FOR AGE OR SKILL LEVEL

- **Beginner:** Premeasure materials and have a station set up for each student when they arrive. Give students an option of two or three figurines.
- **Intermediate:** Place figurines in the middle of the table and encourage students to negotiate who gets which one.
- **Advanced:** Do not have instructions available for students. Encourage students to problem solve how they think they should make the snow globe without giving them any direction. They must surmise how to make it solely based on the materials that are on the table and the model that you have made. Students might think to look up directions online. After

they have attempted to problem solve putting it together before seeking another source, looking up directions or asking another adult might be an appropriate solution.

REFLECTION

The reflection for this activity focuses on how to consider another person's interests and preferences, as well as how to follow a series of steps to complete an activity.

FOLLOW-UP

Decide as a group to play a game, and invite a peer from class. Students in the group can decide what game they should play with others considering (1) what other students like to play and (2) what games are good to play with several people. Other activities that require similar skills include the following:

- Build a Vehicle
- Teacher Appreciation Cards
- Decorate a Door

GENERALIZATION TO THE CLASSROOM

This activity simulates classroom activities in which students are required to follow a specific series of directions to complete a project. It also replicates opportunities in which students have to consider another person's interests over their own.

INSTRUCTOR NOTES AND THOUGHTS

_____
_____
_____
_____
_____
_____

LESSON PLAN EXAMPLE: Snow Globe

Date: _____06/18_____

Activity: _____Snow Globe_____

Students:

_____Thomas_____   _____

_____Joseph_____   _____

_____Katy_____   _____

Materials:

- ☐ Water
- ☐ Small Mason jars
- ☐ Small figurines
- ☐ Glitter (2–3 colors)
- ☐ Pure glycerin
- ☐ Waterproof craft glue
- ☐ Spoons
- ☐ Funnel

Expectations:

- Wash your hands.
- Cooperate with each other.
- Share.
- Help each other.
- Be patient.
- Ask politely.

Steps to Complete:

1. Wash your hands.
2. Decide who to give the snow globe to.
3. Choose a jar.
4. Choose a figurine and check to see if it fits.

5. Glue figurine to the lid.
6. Add glitter to the jar.
7. Add water; check to see if there is enough water.
8. Add glycerin.
9. Glue lid and figurine to the jar.
10. Let it dry.
11. Pick it up at the end of the day.

Successes:

- Thomas helped Joseph find a figurine that would fit into his jar when he saw Joseph become frustrated.
- Katy was thoughtful and explained why she wanted to give it to her sister.
- Students asked to do the activity again and want to make two snow globes: one for a teacher and one for themselves.

Challenges:

- Thomas jumped ahead and put water in before the glitter. He needed to be reminded to follow steps.

Next Time:

- Honor their request to do the activity again, maybe before winter break or for teacher appreciation.

STUDENT REFLECTION: Snow Globe

Date: _____

Activity: _____

Who was here today?

_____   _____

_____   _____

_____   _____

What did you do today?

Today we _____

_____

_____

_____

How did it make you feel?

☐ Satisfied	☐ Frustrated	☐ Bored	☐ _____
☐ Confident	☐ Irritated	☐ Sad	☐ _____
☐ Happy	☐ Anxious	☐ Shy	☐ _____

What did you do well today?

Today I was able to _____

_____

_____

_____

What was the hardest part of the activity?

The hardest part of the activity today was _____

_____

_____

_____

How do you know what other people like?

I know what someone likes because _____

_____

_____

_____

What happens if you do something out of order?

Sometimes, when I do not follow steps, I _____

_____

_____

_____

What can you do in class when you do not get exactly what you want?

In class, I can _____

_____

_____

_____

# SNOW GLOBE

Dakota, a third-grade student, experienced anxiety when presented with difficult tasks because she did not want to make mistakes and look bad. She frequently shut down whenever she felt she made an error and tried to gain attention from adults in maladaptive ways so that they would help her. For example, she would often whine or cry to avoid tasks she perceived as difficult. Many of these avoidance attempts were met with adult support because Dakota was endearing and adults do not like to see kids struggle. However, every time an adult jumped in when she became upset or uncomfortable, her helpless behaviors were reinforced. Dakota needed to learn more appropriate ways to advocate for her needs and increase her frustration tolerance.

When I presented this activity, I shared with the group that we were going to be making a gift and that each person had the opportunity to make one snow globe that they could give to a teacher for Teacher Appreciation Day or to their mother or grandmother for Mother's Day. Dakota immediately asked, "Can I make three?" I told the group that they could only make one snow globe each and that they first needed to decide who they wanted to give it to. Dakota slumped in her chair, put her head down, and began to pout. When I asked her what she needed, she replied, "I can't decide if I should give one to my mom, my teacher, or my grandma. I need to make three because someone will have their feelings hurt." When I reiterated that the group was only going to make one, she began to tear up and said, "Then I won't make one!" I said that it was her decision but that she needed to stay in the room and help her classmates make theirs.

When the other students began choosing their figurines, one boy picked up a small bear, to which Dakota sat up and complained, "I want the bear!" The boy started to hand the bear to her, but I stopped him from doing so, as Dakota often got her way with other students by throwing a bit of a tantrum. I reiterated that the boy had chosen the bear figurine while Dakota was pouting and that his keeping it was fair because he was following the expectations. I told Dakota that if she wanted to make a snow globe, then she had to look at the expectations and choose a figurine from those left on the table. She again began to tear up but chose a small dog and said, "I think my teacher likes dogs."

When it came time to put glitter into their jars, most students carefully sprinkled glitter in. However, two students—one being Dakota—dumped in about two tablespoons of glitter. I did not say anything. When I helped the students fill their jars with water and glycerin, Dakota and the other student noticed that they had too much glitter. Both students became upset because they thought they had ruined their project. Dakota put her snow globe on the table, turned around and folded her arms, and whimpered. The other student attempted to fix her snow globe by dumping out the water so she could start again, and when Dakota saw this, she eventually moved over toward us. After some prompting, she finally asked me, "Can I pour mine out and start over too?" I said,

"Of course." We spent a little time cleaning out the jars as best as we could, and both students asked the other group members how much to put in. After they carefully added a small amount of glitter and water, they could see that their snow globe was now going to work.

This activity presented Dakota with an opportunity to create something that she was excited about, make a mistake, and advocate for herself. She had a chance to see that the mistake was not the end of the world and that she could receive support from an adult simply by asking for help. Despite her discomfort making the snow globe, she was ecstatic to give it to her teacher. During the follow-up session, we talked about how most mistakes can be corrected or adjusted but that we sometimes need to take a small break to problem solve—and sometimes that means asking for help. For Dakota, the reward of presenting something special to her teacher after her struggles was very reinforcing.

Pumpkin Pudding

SUMMARY

The group will be making pudding, which requires students to work together to achieve a goal. This activity also provides students an opportunity to learn some basic life skills so that they can make a treat at home for their family.

OBJECTIVE/GOALS

- Students will collaborate/work together to complete a task.
- Students will follow a sequence of steps to complete a task.

SKILLS SUPPORTED

- Collaboration
- Cooperation
- Following Directions
- Frustration Tolerance
- Impulsivity
- Initiation
- Life Skills
- Listening
- Organization
- Planning
- Problem Solving
- Self-Advocacy
- Sequencing
- Shared Attention
- Taking Turns
- Working Memory

NUMBER OF STUDENTS

- 1–4

MATERIALS

- Large box of instant vanilla pudding
- Large tub of Cool Whip®
- Can of pumpkin puree
- Spices (e.g., pumpkin pie spice, cinnamon, nutmeg)
- Large bowl
- Whisk
- Spoons
- Napkins
- Can opener
- Small individual bowls or cups to eat pudding from

Note: This can be made with or without canned pumpkin and with any flavor pudding and accompanying ingredients.

PREPARATION

__ Check for allergies.

__ Purchase food items.

__ Have all materials ready and placed aside.

__ Create visual with expectations.

__ Create visual with outlined steps.

INTRODUCTION

Students will be making pumpkin pudding together today. This simple dessert has a lot of different flavor options and is something they can make at home with their family. Let students know that they each have to contribute a step to make the pudding and that they will have a chance to eat it together at the end.

EXPECTATIONS

Before you begin, review the expectations for the group and emphasize any behaviors you want to see during the session:

- Wash your hands first.
- Look at ingredients on the table.
- Make a plan together and write it down.
- Decide the order for taking turns.
- Each person must add one ingredient.
- Each person must help stir so that it is all mixed.
- Follow your plan.
- _____
- _____

STEPS

1. Require students to wash their hands.
2. Place materials in the middle of the table but intentionally leave out a tool needed to mix the ingredients together (e.g., bowl or spoon). Students will likely not notice until they need it.
3. Ask students to dictate to you how to make the pudding. See if they look at the box for directions. Because you are using Cool Whip instead of milk, give the students time to look at the materials they have, and encourage them to problem solve how to make the pudding. **This is the brainstorming part of the activity; you are simply the note taker.**

4. Use a board or piece of paper to write down the plan, which should involve a sequence of numbered steps required to make the pudding.

5. Talk through the steps with students, and decide the order in which they will take turns. Remind them that each person has to help make the pudding. Allow them to decide which person will complete each step (e.g., pouring out pudding powder, adding the Cool Whip, stirring, adding spices, etc.), including which person will go first. Sometimes, there are more steps than there are participants, and students will have to problem solve that as well.

6. Allow them to start making the pudding, encouraging them to follow their plan.

7. **When students become stuck, encourage them to problem solve.** For example, when they realize they do not have a tool to mix the ingredients, do not just hand it to them. Rather, make them ask you for it. If you have a kitchen in the building, you can encourage them to look there or ask an adult outside of your room.

8. Require students to take turns mixing, and then serve the pudding into individual bowls. You can allow students to serve themselves (which presents another teaching opportunity because some students will take too much), or you can assign someone to serve each person and have that person serve themselves last.

9. Eat the snack together and reflect on how the activity went.

Note: This activity can present sensory challenges (e.g., texture, smell, etc.). If students have a sensitivity to the texture or taste, let them know that they do not have to eat it. You can have an alternative snack that they can enjoy while their classmates eat the pudding.

CHALLENGES TO INCORPORATE

− Do not have a large bowl on the table.

− Do not have a whisk.

− Do not know how to use a can opener.

+ Add unnecessary ingredients on the table.

+ Try to stick your finger in the bowl.

+ Go out of turn.

+ Start eating before everyone is finished (e.g., break a rule/expectation).

DIFFERENTIATION FOR AGE OR SKILL LEVEL

- **Beginner:** Premeasure ingredients and clearly outline the steps for mixing. Encourage students to ask for help if they become stuck (e.g., using the can opener).

- **Intermediate:** Post vague directions regarding how to complete the task to facilitate problem solving. Do not have all the materials available. If there is a kitchen, encourage students to ask other people in the building for spoons or a can opener. You can also coordinate with another teacher by giving him or her a can opener and encourage students to check that classroom. This helps students learn that if the solution is not right in front of them, they can continue to problem solve and think outside the box.

- **Advanced:** Provide several ingredient options and allow students to invent their own recipe. This will involve more discussion about how to make the pudding. Let students have fun with it! Just remind them that they do have to eat it ☺.

REFLECTION

The reflection for this activity focuses on how to follow steps to complete a task and what types of things students can make at home for snacks.

FOLLOW-UP

Make another simple food or dessert item that follows similar steps, and see if students adjust and generalize from the pudding experience. Take some examples from students' reflection sheets to see what they like to make at home, and ask them to teach their peers. Other activities that require similar skills include the following:

- Friendship Mix
- Ornaments
- Cookie Decorating

GENERALIZATION TO THE CLASSROOM

This activity reflects small-group work in which each student has a responsibility and a way to contribute to the completion of a task. It also provides students with an opportunity to read through directions and come up with a plan before starting a task.

INSTRUCTOR NOTES AND THOUGHTS

_____
_____
_____
_____
_____
_____

LESSON PLAN EXAMPLE: Pumpkin Pudding

Date: _____06/20_____

Activity: _____Pumpkin Pudding_____

Students:

_____Tina_____	_____Sam_____
_____Sasha_____	_____
_____Torah_____	_____

Materials:

Food

- ☐ Large box of instant vanilla pudding
- ☐ Large tub of Cool Whip
- ☐ Can of pumpkin puree
- ☐ Spices (e.g., pumpkin spice, cinnamon, nutmeg)

Other

- ☐ Large bowl
- ☐ Whisk
- ☐ Napkins
- ☐ Spoons
- ☐ Can opener

Expectations:

- Wash your hands first.
- Plan together.
- Each person must add one ingredient.
- Each person must help stir so it is all mixed.
- Follow your plan.
- Eat.

Steps to Complete:

1. Wash your hands first.
2. Look at ingredients on the table.
3. Make a plan for how to make the pudding and write it down.
4. Decide the order for taking turns.

5. Add one ingredient at a time.

6. Take turns stirring until it's all mixed.

7. Split into even servings.

8. Eat.

Successes:

- Sasha took on a leadership role and made sure everyone had a turn in order.
- Sam asked for help using the can opener before he got really frustrated.

Challenges:

- Tina was uncomfortable with the texture of the pudding and did not look at it. She needed support staying in the room.

Next Time:

- Consider the texture and smell involved in the cooking activity, and prepare students ahead of time for what they will have to do to participate.
- Help Tina stay in her seat and work through what she does not like with support.

STUDENT REFLECTION: Pumpkin Pudding

Date:_____

Activity:_____

Who was here today?

_____   _____
_____   _____
_____   _____

What did you do today?

Today we _____
_____
_____
_____

How did it make you feel?

- ☐ Satisfied
- ☐ Confident
- ☐ Happy
- ☐ Frustrated
- ☐ Irritated
- ☐ Anxious
- ☐ Bored
- ☐ Sad
- ☐ Shy
- ☐ _____
- ☐ _____
- ☐ _____

What did you do well today?

Today I was able to _____
_____
_____
_____

What was the hardest part of the activity?

The hardest part of the activity today was _____
_____
_____
_____

What will you do differently next time?

Next time, I will _____

_____

_____

_____

Can you still make pudding if you do any of the steps out of order?   Yes   No

Why or why not?

_____

_____

_____

Why is it important to follow directions in order?

It is important to follow directions in order because _____

_____

_____

_____

What happens when you read all the directions before you start?

When I read through directions before I start _____

_____

_____

_____

What types of snacks can you make at home for you and your family?

At home, I can make _____

_____

_____

_____

PUMPKIN PUDDING

Jack, a sixth-grade student diagnosed with autism, often had difficulty managing his emotional reactions to unpredictable situations. When he became uncomfortable with situations in the classroom, he would often leave, which required teachers to spend a lot of time looking for him in the school building, calming him down, and problem solving/debriefing regarding what to do when unpredictable situations arise.

During the first few months of school, Christie Bowers and I worked with Jack to increase his vocabulary, identify his feelings, learn effective strategies for calming down, and teach him how to appropriately advocate for his needs when he was uncomfortable. Around Thanksgiving, we decided to do a joint activity that involved making pumpkin pudding. When Christie pulled out the Cool Whip, Jack yelled, "No!" and ran out of the room. We did not know it at the time, but Jack had a sensitivity to the texture of Cool Whip. After finding Jack and helping him calm down, we called his mother, and she shared that Jack had an adverse reaction to things like whipped cream and that he would never eat it or touch it.

Christie and I decided to attempt the activity again. We prepped Jack by letting him know in advance that we were going to make pudding again. He was resistant at first, but once we gave him a job (to get the bowls), he felt prepared and was willing to attempt the activity. Our goal was to help him manage his reaction and emotions while staying in the classroom. During this second attempt, when the Cool Whip came out, Jack gagged and moved his chair toward the door, but he stayed in the classroom for the entire activity! We attempted the activity a third time with a little less support, and Jack was able to stir the pudding before his classmates ate it.

The point of the entire activity was never for Jack to eat pudding or to even make pudding. The goal was to challenge Jack in a small way and in a safe environment so that he could work through his challenges, manage his emotions, and actively engage in the activity. When something like this arose in his classroom, he was now able to rely on his experience of staying in the classroom during the pudding activity and receiving adult support rather than running away.

Teacher Appreciation Cards

SUMMARY

This activity takes several sessions (at least three) to complete and can be done for any holiday. Each session is broken down to simulate writing tasks that occur in the classroom environment, as well as to teach students how to follow a sequence of steps to complete a project. This activity requires more modeling from you as the instructor, but it is intended to look like a process in the classroom. You are also encouraged to collaborate with the students' teachers to support the process that is being taught in the classroom.

OBJECTIVE/GOALS

- Students will preplan and follow a sequence of steps to complete a long-term project.
- Students will demonstrate flexibility.
- Students will identify factors/circumstances that cause frustration and stress.

SKILLS SUPPORTED

- Collaboration
- Emotion Regulation
- Expressive Language
- Flexibility
- Following Directions
- Frustration Tolerance/Perseverance
- Impulsivity
- Initiation
- Organization
- Planning
- Problem Solving
- Self-Advocacy
- Sequencing
- Taking Turns
- Theory of Mind

NUMBER OF STUDENTS

- 1–6

MATERIALS

- White paper
- Colored construction paper
- Pencils
- Markers
- Stickers
- Glitter
- Glue

PREPARATION

__ Collaborate with classroom teacher(s) to support writing steps taught in class.
__ Collect needed materials from around the school (you should not need to purchase additional items).
__ Create a template for the students to follow.
__ Create a rough draft of a Teacher Appreciation Card.
__ Create a final example of a Teacher Appreciation Card that follows your rough draft.

INTRODUCTION

When Teacher Appreciation Day is a few weeks away, ask students to make some cards to say, "Thank You!" to their teachers. Share with students that the project will take a few weeks and that they will have to follow the steps of making a rough draft, followed by a final draft. Show students your final product, and take some time to discuss the differences between a rough draft and a final draft and why you have both. Students must include three to five sentences on their card, and the group will brainstorm sentences together to put on the cards. The rough draft will not have any decorations on it, so encourage students to think about how they want to incorporate decorations onto their draft. Students will deliver their cards to their teachers during Teacher Appreciation Week.

EXPECTATIONS

Before you begin, review the expectations for the group and emphasize any behaviors you want to see during the session:

- Listen to directions.
- Brainstorm ideas together.
- Follow directions/steps.
- Be patient (the rough draft is not supposed to be perfect).
- Share materials.
- Must include three to five sentences.
- Use rough draft to guide final product (e.g., they should be similar).
- _____
- _____

STEPS

Session 1: Brainstorm

1. Discuss making Teacher Appreciation Cards.
2. Show students your final product.
3. Get out a calendar and look at what day Teacher Appreciation Day will be.
4. Ask students how long they think it will take to make the cards. Encourage three sessions.

Teacher Appreciation Cards 49

5. Help students decide which teacher they want to give a card to. Older students should create more than one.

6. Create a simple template on the board for students to include on their cards, such as:

   Dear _____,

   Thank you for _____.

   I like that you _____.

   You are a great teacher because _____.

7. Brainstorm some words, sentences, and adjectives that students can include on their card. As students brainstorm aloud, take notes on the board to summarize students' ideas in writing.

8. Once you are done brainstorming, provide students with a piece of white paper, and let them know that it will serve as their rough draft.

9. Ask them to fold the paper in half and decide which direction they want their card (e.g., vertical or horizontal).

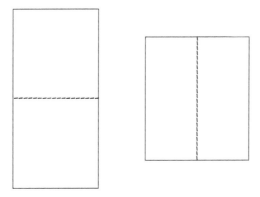

10. Tell students that they will be working on their rough draft during the next session.

11. Ask students to write their name down on the piece of paper. Then, collect the folded pieces of paper from each student, and take a picture of the brainstorming board so you can re-create it next time before students come in.

Session 2: Rough Draft

1. Re-create the brainstorming board you made during the first session.

2. Display your rough draft example so students can refer to it.

3. Pass out the folded paper from the previous week.

4. Remind students to include three to five sentences on the card. You can differentiate the number of sentences to include on the card based on students' age and writing ability.

5. Instruct students to start making their rough draft, and reiterate that it does not have to be perfect. The rough draft is supposed to be a broad, general idea for their card; they will add details on their final draft. For students who have

accommodations that allow them to type or dictate instead of write, be sure to have such supports available.

6. Let students know that they will be able to decorate their final card with color, stickers, and so on but that this draft will only include writing. Encourage them to think about how they want to decorate their final card.

7. Encourage students to cross things out, erase, and/or rewrite what they want on their card. Often, students will want the rough draft to be the best draft so that they can skip the next step in making the final card or because they have a hard time being flexible with what a rough draft is intended to be. Some students will have a very hard time creating a rough draft and will want to start over several times. **These students will need support managing themselves, working through mistakes, and being flexible.**

8. Once the rough drafts are complete, facilitate a discussion to discuss the best time and place to deliver their cards to the teacher. Having this discussion during the second session is best so that students are prepared to deliver their final card when it is complete.

9. Collect the rough drafts for the next session.

Session 3: Final Card

1. Pass out the rough drafts that were completed at the previous session.

2. Spread out a variety of materials on the table (e.g., colored paper, stickers, markers, glitter) that students can use to decorate their final card.

3. Ask students to choose a piece of colored construction paper for their final card.

4. Instruct students to use their rough draft to guide them in completing their final card. Although you can allow students to make small changes, remind them that the cards need to look similar. **Students will often want to make something completely different than their rough draft, but do *not* allow them to re-create a completely different card.** Allowing them to do so will not support them in developing planning and organizational skills. This activity is intended to support the specific process of creating a rough draft that includes broad ideas, followed by a final draft that includes final details, which is often a process that is utilized in the classroom.

5. Once students have written the message on the card, allow them to decorate the card however they would like.

CHALLENGES TO INCORPORATE

– Provide less support with brainstorming.

– Do not have all the necessary materials.

– Only allow two pieces of paper for rough draft mistakes (no infinite do-overs).

+ Stop a student from starting over on his or her rough draft.

DIFFERENTIATION FOR AGE OR SKILL LEVEL

- **Beginner:** Outline the sentence structure for the inside of the card, and brainstorm adjectives for students to fill in. Consulting with the classroom teacher will give you the best way to present the activity successfully and to ensure that you are supporting the skill required for writing.

- **Intermediate:** Require the students to figure out what materials they need during the first session. During this session, ask the students what materials they will need and where they think they can get them (e.g., ask the art teacher, bring in themselves, etc.). The materials should be available in the school, so facilitate a discussion regarding how students can best get what they need. They, or you, may need to volunteer to bring in something (e.g., stickers).

- **Advanced:** Students can be more independent with the creation of the card or in coming up with a gesture to show appreciation. They may want to make the cards on the computer or some other way. The point is teacher appreciation, so encourage students to come up with an appropriate gesture or way to show their teachers that they are appreciated.

REFLECTION

The reflection for this activity focuses on the importance of planning ahead and following a specified plan.

FOLLOW-UP

Given that Mother's Day is very close to Teacher Appreciation Week, you can follow up by having students create a Mother's Day card but with fewer steps outlined. You can also encourage older students to bring in a long-term assignment and have them work with the group to create an outline for when and how to complete the assignment. Other activities that require similar skills include the following:

- Build a Vehicle
- Cookie Decorating
- Decorate a Door
- Build a Bridge

GENERALIZATION TO THE CLASSROOM

This activity emulates classroom activities where students have to think ahead, create a draft, and then develop a final product. It provides them experience with chunking tasks and managing their time to complete a long-term project.

INSTRUCTOR NOTES AND THOUGHTS

LESSON PLAN EXAMPLE:
Teacher Appreciation Cards

Date: _____04/23_____

Activity: __Teacher Appreciation Cards____

Students:

_____Jessica_____	_____Marcus_____
_____Tonya_____	_____Gabe_____
_____Cody_____	_____

Materials:

- ☐ White paper
- ☐ Colored construction paper
- ☐ Pencils
- ☐ Markers
- ☐ Stickers
- ☐ Glitter
- ☐ Glue

Expectations:

- Listen to directions.
- Brainstorm ideas together.
- Be patient—rough drafts have mistakes.
- Follow the steps in order.
- Share materials.
- Include 3 to 5 sentences.

Steps to Complete:

1. Check the calendar to see when Teacher Appreciation Day is.
2. Look at the example cards.
3. Decide how long it will take to get the cards completed on time and set a schedule.
4. Decide which teacher you want to make a card for.
5. Brainstorm words and sentences that you can put on the card.

6. Make a rough draft.
7. Make a final draft.
8. Deliver the card.

Successes:
- All cards were completed, and students were proud to give them to their teachers.
- Marcus asked to type his card on the computer.

Challenges:
- Jessica became very upset when she was encouraged to erase her mistakes on the rough draft instead of starting over. She needed support to work through her emotions and try again.
- Cody refused to participate during the brainstorming session.

Next Time:
- Provide Cody with a word bank so he can participate in brainstorming.
- Try making cards for Mother's Day.

STUDENT REFLECTION:
Teacher Appreciation Cards

Date: _____

Activity: _____

Who was here today?

_____   _____

_____   _____

_____   _____

What did you do today?

Today we _____

_____

_____

_____

How did it make you feel?

- ☐ Satisfied
- ☐ Confident
- ☐ Happy

- ☐ Frustrated
- ☐ Irritated
- ☐ Anxious

- ☐ Bored
- ☐ Sad
- ☐ Shy

- ☐ _____
- ☐ _____
- ☐ _____

What did you do well today?

Today I was able to _____

_____

_____

_____

What was the hardest part of the activity?

The hardest part of the activity today was _____

_____

_____

_____

What will you do differently next time?

Next time, I will _____

_____

_____

_____

Why is it helpful to have a plan before you start a project?

It is helpful to have a plan before you start a project because _____

_____

_____

_____

When is it helpful to create a rough draft?

A rough draft is helpful when _____

_____

_____

_____

TEACHER APPRECIATION CARDS

One year, I completed this activity with a group of fifth-grade students who had difficulty organizing and communicating their thoughts and managing their emotions when things did not go their way. In particular, the students in this group often had a very difficult time following multistep directions, initiating tasks, staying focused, and completing their work on time. A common theme in their IEP meetings was that homework often took hours and led to tears, and their parents were beyond frustrated because they were afraid of the additional challenges middle school would bring. Throughout the year, I had tasked the group with learning how to manage multistep projects and advocate for themselves because those were important skills they would need when entering middle school. We worked on how to break assignments down into smaller parts, and we practiced using task sheets and graphic organizers to get their ideas on paper and create an outline. I presented the Teacher Appreciation Cards activity as a way of reinforcing how to dissect a larger project into a series of more manageable steps.

When I first presented this activity to the group, the students were very excited to make a card for their teacher, but they wanted to dive in, write a simple note, and give it to their teacher right away. I reiterated that we were going to make a rough draft first, which required that they think about how they wanted the card to look and to brainstorm what types of things they wanted to say. I also set the expectation that they would include at least four sentences. As I continued to outline the expectations, the enthusiasm for creating a card for their teacher waned. I brought out my example that was decorated with a lot of glitter and stickers, and the students perked up a little. We began brainstorming different ways to say thank you, and I asked the students to share what characteristics about their teacher they appreciated. We were able to develop a long list of adjectives, as well as some simple sentence starters.

The following week, I gave the students blank pieces of paper and pencils and let them know they were required to create a rough draft; I intentionally had pencils that did not have erasers. The students really wanted to add decorations to their rough draft, but I reminded them that this draft would only include writing. Most of the students wrote "Happy Teacher Appreciation Day" on the front of their card and paused before they began writing on the inside. I encouraged them to think about what they wanted to put down before they began writing because they were required to write at least four sentences. As each student started their first sentence, I started hearing, "Ugh"; "Oh man, that's not right"; and "Wait, I messed up. I need a new piece of paper!" I reiterated that this was a draft and that there was no need for a new piece of paper. I suggested that they cross out their mistakes, which led to several meltdowns. I needed to provide a significant amount of support to one student in particular, Jesse, who refused to cross something out and ripped her card in half. I encouraged the other students in the group to refer to the whiteboard with all our brainstorming ideas and to continue with their draft while I helped Jesse.

As I worked with Jesse to identify what was frustrating her, she admitted that she hated crossing things out or having eraser marks on her paper. We came up with a solution for her to dictate her ideas to me so I could write them down, and she then transferred those ideas onto a new piece of paper. I still gave her a pencil without an eraser, and when she made a mistake, we took a deep breath together as she crossed out a word. I did not realize it at the time, but Jesse's mom later shared with me that it often took her hours to write a single paragraph. After learning that, I realized what a success it was that Jesse was willing and able to work through her frustrations by crossing out her mistakes and moving forward to make a great card for her teacher.

For the third session, I provided students with fun decorations, redistributed the draft cards, and encouraged them to add any embellishments they wanted. I did remind them that their final draft needed to be similar to the rough draft. One student made several attempts to change a few sentences but was redirected easily. As the students decorated their cards, we talked about how most of the work involved in completing a final project is done on the front end during the process of brainstorming and creating rough drafts. They agreed that the final step of this activity was relatively easy and fun to complete because they had put down all their ideas on paper beforehand. Overall, they learned that by having a detailed plan ahead of time, they were able to stay on task, which allowed them to spend the last part of the activity adding fun details and making it look how they wanted—and they could also complete it on time.

Ornaments

SUMMARY

Students will be making an ornament to hang in their house or give to someone. This activity requires students to follow multistep directions and adjust their approach to completing a task based on what they see and feel. It is a great activity that can be done before a holiday and teaches students how to follow a very simple recipe. This activity can also be successfully completed with students with significant needs because there are very few steps and few verbal communication requirements. The recipe included makes four to six ornaments.

OBJECTIVE/GOALS

- Students will follow multistep directions successfully.
- Students will adjust their plan based on what they see and feel.
- Students will share resources with others and take turns.

SKILLS SUPPORTED

- Cooperation
- Flexibility
- Following Directions
- Frustration Tolerance
- Impulsivity
- Initiation
- Life Skills
- Listening
- Organization
- Planning
- Problem Solving
- Self-Advocacy
- Sequencing
- Shared Attention
- Taking Turns

NUMBER OF STUDENTS

- 1–4

MATERIALS

- 1 cup unsweetened applesauce
- 1½ cups ground cinnamon
- 2 tablespoons of glue
- Mixing bowl
- Measuring spoons and cups

- Rolling pin
- Plastic wrap
- Cookie cutters
- Straw
- Spatula
- Cookie tray
- String or ribbon
- Glitter or other decoration items

PREPARATION

__ Check for allergies to applesauce or spices.

__ Purchase the items.

__ Make a model/final product to show students.

__ Create visual with expectations.

__ Create visual with outlined steps.

INTRODUCTION

Students will be making an ornament to hang in their house. They will have to work together to create the base material made of applesauce, glue, and spices. Sometimes, the consistency does not turn out right; it can be too thin and runny or too thick to roll out and cut. They will have to make some adjustments based on what they see and feel. The ornaments they end up making will smell great, but they are *not* edible. Once students have made their ornaments, they will need to leave them to dry and pick them up later in the week. If you plan to have the students decorate them, it will take two sessions to complete.

EXPECTATIONS

Before you begin, review the expectations for the group and emphasize any behaviors you want to see during the session:

- Wash your hands.
- Look at the materials and think of what type of ornament you want to make.
- Follow directions and work together.
- Help each other if someone gets stuck.
- Share.
- Be patient.
- Ask politely.
- _____
- _____

STEPS

1. Require students to wash their hands.
2. Show the students your final ornament.
3. Place materials in the middle of the table.
4. Ask students to follow the recipe and mix together the applesauce, cinnamon, and glue in a bowl.
5. Encourage all of them to try kneading the dough with their hands until it is smooth. If it is too sticky, add more cinnamon. If it is too dry, add more applesauce.
6. Divide the dough into sections so that each student has a small ball.
7. Encourage students to pat their ball into a flat shape so it is approximately ¼ to ½ inch thick. Make sure that the flattened dough is large enough for the cookie cutter to form it into the desired shape.
8. Press the cookie cutter into the dough and pull the excess off the sides.
9. Pull the cookie cutter away from the counter.
10. Make a hole in the top of the dough with a straw or pencil.
11. Carefully use a spatula to remove the ornament from the table, and place it on a cookie sheet to dry. You should leave them out to dry for a few days, making sure to flip them occasionally.
12. When the ornaments are dry, insert a ribbon in the hole and tie it in a knot.
13. If desired, you can use a second session to decorate the ornaments.

Note: This activity can present sensory challenges (e.g., texture, smell, etc.). If students have a sensitivity to the texture of the dough, encourage them to use utensils to stir it, manipulate it, and roll it out. If they have a sensitivity to the smell, have other options they can try, such as clove, nutmeg, and so on. You can also add flour instead to have no smell; just be sure it is a dry powder.

CHALLENGES TO INCORPORATE

− Do not have all materials necessary to complete the project.

+ Add too much applesauce.

+ Have unnecessary ingredients on the table (see if they question it).

DIFFERENTIATION FOR AGE OR SKILL LEVEL

- **Beginner:** Follow the steps as is. Students may need some help kneading the dough and rolling it out to the right thickness.
- **Intermediate:** Add small challenges and do not provide help until someone asks. If the students do not roll the dough out to the correct thickness, or if they add too much applesauce, you can problem solve with them when they notice that the ornament does not dry or is too flimsy.

- **Advanced:** Show the students your final ornament and give them the three ingredients (e.g., applesauce, glue, and cinnamon), but do not tell them how much of each ingredient to use. Let them experiment to find the right consistency. See if and when they ask for help. This approach also leads to a great discussion.

REFLECTION

Reflection for this activity focuses on following a recipe to make something correctly and figuring out what to do when things are not turning out as expected.

FOLLOW-UP

This activity can easily be generalized to any other simple recipe that requires following directions. You can find some simple food recipes online that do not require an oven. You can also help students look up simple recipes online, print them, and take them home so that they can try to expand on what they can cook for themselves at home. Consult with their parents so students have some support at home. The following are other activities that require similar skills:

- Pumpkin Pudding
- Cookie Decorating
- Friendship Mix

GENERALIZATION TO THE CLASSROOM

This activity simulates classroom activities in which students are required to follow a specific series of directions to complete a project. It is also a great activity to facilitate conversations with parents about how to incorporate cooking with their child at home so they can learn this important life skill.

INSTRUCTOR NOTES AND THOUGHTS

_____
_____
_____
_____
_____
_____

LESSON PLAN EXAMPLE: Ornaments

Date: _____12/17_____

Activity: _____Ornaments_____

Students:

_____Michael_____	_____Allie_____
_____Patrick_____	_____
_____Jesse_____	_____

Materials:

- ☐ Applesauce
- ☐ Liquid glue
- ☐ Cinnamon
- ☐ Bowl
- ☐ Measuring spoons and cups
- ☐ Cookie cutters
- ☐ Rolling pin
- ☐ Cookie sheet
- ☐ Straw/pencil
- ☐ Spatula
- ☐ Ribbon/string

Expectations:

- Wash your hands.
- Look at the materials and think of what you want to make.
- Follow directions and work together.
- Help each other if someone gets stuck.
- Share.
- Be patient.
- Ask politely.

Steps to Complete:

1. Wash your hands first.
2. Look at the completed ornament.
3. Measure out your ingredients.
4. Place ingredients in a bowl and mix with your hands.

5. Check the consistency.
6. Divide the dough so each person has a small ball.
7. Roll out your ball so you can place a cookie cutter on it.
8. Press the cookie cutter onto your rolled dough.
9. Peel away the extra dough.
10. Push a hole at the top with a straw.
11. Carefully place your ornament on a cookie sheet to dry.
12. Let the ornament dry and come pick it up in a few days.
13. Tie a ribbon in the hole when it is dry.

Successes:
- Michael figured out that the dough was too wet, and Jesse suggested that we add some dry things.

Challenges:
- Patrick did not want to touch the dough with his hands and refused to try something else for five minutes.

Next Time:
- Brainstorm ways we can mix things if we are uncomfortable with touching slimy or sticky things, and practice with utensils or gloves.

STUDENT REFLECTION: Ornaments

Date: _____

Activity: _____

Who was here today?

_____   _____

_____   _____

_____   _____

What did you do today?

Today we _____

_____

_____

_____

How did it make you feel?

- ☐ Satisfied
- ☐ Confident
- ☐ Happy
- ☐ Frustrated
- ☐ Irritated
- ☐ Anxious
- ☐ Bored
- ☐ Sad
- ☐ Shy
- ☐ _____
- ☐ _____
- ☐ _____

What did you do well today?

Today I was able to _____

_____

_____

_____

What was the hardest part of the activity?

The hardest part of the activity today was _____

_____

_____

_____

Have you ever followed a recipe before?   Yes   No

What happens when someone messes up following a recipe?

When someone messes up a recipe, _____
_____
_____
_____

How do you handle it when you try to make something and it does not turn out the way you expected it to?

When things do not turn out the way I expect, I _____
_____
_____
_____

What are some simple recipes you can try at home?

At home, I can make _____
_____
_____
_____

List of suggested recipes for home:
- Brownies
- Cupcakes
- Mac and Cheese
- Oatmeal
- Smoothies
- _____
- _____

 ORNAMENTS

Given that this activity is particularly useful when working with students with significant needs, I often complete this activity with Christie Bowers and another paraprofessional as well. In one particular instance, we had three students who were mostly nonverbal in the group, with one student requiring hand-over-hand support. Prior to starting the activity, we had made sample ornaments for each student to have in front of them, and Christie had created a visual set of directions that were very simplified and included real pictures for each step. With our adult–student ratio, we were able to have one adult support for each student, and we slowly went through each step together, with an adult modeling the action before requiring the student to complete the step.

We spent a lot of time focusing on how to measure ingredients, showing the students the different measuring cups and spoons and how to fill them appropriately. One student measured and added the applesauce, another student measured and added the cinnamon, and the third measured and added the glue. I stirred the ingredients together while Christie reviewed what we had completed and what was going to happen next. Once the mixture came together, I sectioned it off and gave each student a small amount. We showed the students how to roll out their dough and encouraged them to select a cookie cutter to press into their dough. Although the students needed some support kneading the dough and rolling it out, they were able to practice some of their fine motor skills. Some students even made two ornaments, and they beamed when we helped them pull away the rest of the dough and they saw their gingerbread men and snowmen ornaments.

Although this activity can typically be done in one session, we broke up this activity into two sessions to ensure that the students received enough support at each step and because we also wanted to give them a chance to decorate their ornaments. For the second session, we prepared smaller amounts of glue, glitter, and beads in small plastic cups so students could easily access whatever materials they wanted to use to decorate their ornament without struggling to manipulate larger containers. Then, we placed their dried ornaments in front of them, stepped back, and gave them the freedom to add the desired finishing touches to their ornaments. The students all paused, seemingly unsure of how to proceed, until we encouraged them to go ahead with the decorations. They then began decorating their ornaments fairly independently and with much less support required from us. The student who required hand-over-hand assistance did need help reaching for and picking up the decoration items, but Christie worked with her to communicate which items she wanted to use.

Once the other two students started, they never once looked up at us for guidance as they dove into their decorations. This display of independence was important to me because, in class, they would not initiate a task or move through a task without looking to an adult for help first. Watching the mess taking place was a little hard, requiring some restraint on my part, but I used it as an opportunity to model for the paraprofessional that we did not need to step in to support students every time we were uneasy about a task. Each student ended up using every ounce of every decoration—whether on the ornament or on the floor—and smiled proudly as holding up their masterpieces for us to see. We then invited their teacher into the room so they could show her as well. Through this dual-session activity, not only did students learn how to complete a multistep project with assistance from us, but they also learned they that did not always need to look to an adult for guidance to successfully complete a task on their own.

Card or Board Games

SUMMARY

A variety of available card or board games will allow you to facilitate the development of social skills among students. Age-appropriate games are a great way to teach children about initiating and maintaining social interactions, as well as to demonstrate activities that they can do with their peer group. Games also provide you an opportunity to insert various social challenges that students are likely to face daily. By intentionally incorporating challenges in the context of the game, you present students with difficulties that they will have to manage when interacting with their peers in real-life social situations.

This activity outline is the most basic because it can be applied to *any* game you choose to play, and it gives you the flexibility to add games into your sessions that fit your agenda. However, it also requires that you be flexible and aware of all the behaviors that may need support at any one given time. You can choose to make the game as simple or as complex as you would like. Age-appropriate games can be intermixed between sessions and provide students with opportunities to practice their learned skills to interact successfully with others.

OBJECTIVE/GOALS

- Students will collaborate and negotiate with their peers.
- Students will be flexible.
- Students will demonstrate good sportsmanship/graciousness in winning or losing.

SKILLS SUPPORTED

- Cooperation
- Emotion Regulation
- Flexibility
- Following Directions
- Frustration Tolerance
- Impulsivity
- Initiation
- Life Skills
- Listening
- Locus of Control
- Planning
- Problem Solving
- Recognizing Nonverbal Cues
- Self-Advocacy
- Self-Regulation
- Sequencing
- Shared Attention
- Taking Turns
- Theory of Mind
- Working Memory

NUMBER OF STUDENTS

- 1–6

MATERIALS

Any age-appropriate card or board game, such as the following:

- UNO
- Apples to Apples®
- Heads Up!
- Candy Land®
- Sorry!®
- MindTrap®
- Battleship®
- Guess Who?®
- Blockus
- Qwirkle®

PREPARATION

__ Choose a game beforehand, OR

__ Choose a few games to have available and make the students compromise and select.

INTRODUCTION

Students will be playing a game of choice. Remind them that they will be required to work together and, *as always*, that you will be adding challenges and/or new rules so that they can practice problem solving and managing their emotions.

EXPECTATIONS

Before you begin, review the expectations for the group and emphasize any behaviors you want to see during the session:

- Work together.
- Compromise (this activity provides a good chance to talk about what it means).
- Be patient.
- Know when it is your turn.
- Wait your turn.
- Follow the rules.
- _____
- _____

STEPS

1. Present students with two choices of games.
2. Ask students to decide which game they would like to play that day. **If there is a disagreement regarding the choice of game, it may take a while until the group determines the fairest way to come to a decision. Do not intervene!** Allow the students to work through their disagreements to come to a conclusion, even if it takes the majority of the session time. Learning how to compromise is particularly useful for students who are inflexible. See if they come up with a compromise on their own or if a student just gives in.
3. Let students know that they have to follow the rules that are set out by you or that they have agreed on at the beginning. Often, students have a preconceived notion for how to play the game (and slight differences in their understanding of how the game is supposed to be played) based on their previous experience. For example, when playing the game UNO, some children choose one card from the pile if they do not have one to play, whereas others insist that they have to keep choosing cards from the pile until they find a card they can play. **Do not necessarily intervene as students try to negotiate how the game is *supposed* to be played.**
4. Ask the students to decide who should go first and see what strategy they come up with. Sometimes, students will decide through rock, paper, scissors, but there are a lot of other ways too. This is a great opportunity for students to learn that, when they play with a group, they do not always get to go first just because they want to.
5. Begin playing the game, and incorporate challenges as you see fit.

Note: There will be multiple "teachable" moments presented to you throughout every single game. Choose your moments and see if the students generalize what they learn the next time you present them with another game.

CHALLENGES TO INCORPORATE

− Do not discuss the rules before starting.

+ Be adamant on the choice of game instead of allowing students to choose.

+ Cheat.

+ Win.

ı Make up a random rule.

+ Allow a student to make up a random rule.

+ Interrupt.

+ Go out of order/turn.

+ Incorporate a team aspect.

DIFFERENTIATION FOR AGE OR SKILL LEVEL

- **Beginner:** Pick one game. Read the directions first so all the students know the expectations.
- **Intermediate:** Do not read the directions before you begin. Ask a student to make up an additional rule that the group has to follow.

- **Advanced:** Ask students to bring in a favorite or preferred game and teach the group how to play. Require one student to be the leader of the group while you be a player.

REFLECTION

Reflections for any game should focus on the challenges you observed throughout the game. Remember to always include a discussion about what the students did well and how what they did relates to social interactions outside of your group.

FOLLOW-UP

Repeat the same game, but include different challenges or allow students to bring in some games to share with others. Other activities that require similar skills include the following:

- Friendship Mix
- Build a Vehicle
- Decorate a Door
- Scavenger Hunt

GENERALIZATION TO THE CLASSROOM

This activity simulates unstructured social situations that students encounter in the context of the classroom environment and provides them with practice playing games with others. It also provides opportunities to manage themselves with something that is less predictable. You can also take this as an opportunity to teach and practice games that students can play with their peers.

INSTRUCTOR NOTES AND THOUGHTS

_____
_____
_____
_____
_____
_____

LESSON PLAN EXAMPLE:
Card or Board Games

Date: _____12/22_____

Activity: _____Apples to Apples_____

Students:

_____Heather_____	_____Catherine_____
_____Becky_____	_____Jade_____
_____Jackie_____	_____

Materials:

☐ Apples to Apples

Expectations:

- Work together.
- Compromise.
- Wait your turn.
- Be patient.
- Know when it is your turn.

Steps to Complete:

1. Choose a game.
2. Decide the rules of the game.
3. Decide who goes first.
4. Play the game.

Successes:

- Jade utilized self-talk to stay focused.
- All students read through the green word together and understood the vocabulary once the examples were read.
- Becky encouraged Heather when Heather got frustrated and offered Heather a solution.

Challenges:

- Heather yelled, "I never get my card picked!"
- When I cheated, all the students stared at me and did not say anything.

Next Time:

- Discuss how to approach a situation when you see someone cheat or be unfair.
- Insert another challenge that facilitates simple advocacy or confrontation.

STUDENT REFLECTION: Card or Board Games

Date: _____

Activity: _____

Who was here today?

_____   _____

_____   _____

_____   _____

What did you do today?

Today we _____

_____

_____

_____

How did it make you feel?

- ☐ Satisfied
- ☐ Confident
- ☐ Happy
- ☐ Frustrated
- ☐ Irritated
- ☐ Anxious
- ☐ Bored
- ☐ Sad
- ☐ Shy
- ☐ _____
- ☐ _____
- ☐ _____

What did you do well today?

Today I was able to _____

_____

_____

_____

What was the hardest part of the activity?

The hardest part of the activity today was _____

_____

_____

_____

What games do other kids like to play?

Other kids like to play _____

_____

_____

_____

When you are playing with other children, do you always get to choose the game?

Yes   No

When you are playing with other kids, how does the group decide what to play?

When I am playing with other kids, we decide what to play by _____

_____

_____

_____

How can you advocate for yourself if you do not like the game?

If I do not like the game or do not want to play, I can _____

_____

_____

_____

How do you know if you are being a good sport?

A good sport _____

_____

_____

_____

What will you do differently next time?

Next time, I will _____

_____

_____

_____

CARD OR BOARD GAMES

One year, I was working with a new group of sixth-grade students who were all diagnosed with autism spectrum disorder. After they had become comfortable with one another, I shared that we were going to start playing some games and doing activities when they came to my room. We had a fun discussion about some of their favorite games, many of which included video games. When I shared that my favorite video game is Super Mario Brothers 3, one student looked directly at me and said, "Oh my God, Dr. Mak, that game is like from the '80s. How old are you?" Another student added, "Oh yeah, that game console is awesome. I collect the vintage ones." Normally, this would have been a teachable moment, but I was laughing too hard.

Although I told them that playing video games would not be part of our school activities, this discussion allowed me to learn about some of their interests, which provided insight into what types of games we could play that would help them participate in social activities with their same-age peers. During one of our sessions together, I pulled out the game UNO and asked the students if they knew how to play. All of them said that they did, so I proceeded by asking one student to deal out the cards. As the student started dealing the cards, he gave himself six cards, and then dealt six cards to the person next to him, and so on until each of us had six cards. One student commented, "That is not how you deal cards," and another commented, "You're supposed to give us seven cards!" The students began to argue, and one student eventually looked at me and said, "I am right ... right?" I said I did not know because we never decided what the rules were before we began the game. The students just froze and looked at me, so I encouraged them to put their cards down and have a brief discussion about how many cards they needed to start the game. I also modeled for the first student (e.g., the dealer) how he could deal out cards one at a time per person. The students decided to start with seven cards each and that the person to the right of the dealer was to go first.

The first few rounds went smoothly until one student placed a red "Draw Two" on the pile. The student who followed that card drew two from the deck and then placed a red "eight" on the pile. One student immediately yelled, "You can't do that! You are supposed to draw two, and then your turn is over!" The student who had recently placed the red card down replied, "That's how I play at my house," and another student said, "Yeah, that's how I play too." The students again began arguing, and I intervened by asking, "If we all play differently at home, how should we decide how we play here?" All the students froze until one student said, "We can read the directions." I told them I had lost the directions and that we needed to come up with the rules for the game ourselves.

After a very long pause, I started by asking what the basic rules were for the game. The students began talking about rules related to matching colors or numbers, to which I replied, "What about when you don't have a color or number to put down?" All the students chimed in saying that you had to draw from the deck, and I asked, "How many?" The group decided that you had to draw until you got a card you could play, and then you were allowed to put it on the pile. After we established some of these basic rules,

I wrote them down on the whiteboard, and we began to play again. Each time a new card was placed on the pile that we had not discussed (e.g., skip, reverse, etc.), I stopped the game until we came up with a solution for how to proceed.

At the end of the first UNO session, I reflected with the students that establishing expectations before beginning an activity is often a good idea and that anytime they are in my room, they will be expected to work together, ask questions, and problem solve. I also told them that although we would be doing a lot of fun activities together, they were not going to be easy. They would need to learn how be flexible, and all I would ever ask is that they try.

After introducing UNO a few more times, the students quickly changed their behaviors when they became irritated or confused. Often, they would ask to put a new rule or expectation on the board so it was set in stone, and they would refer to the board immediately when they entered the room. They also became accustomed to receiving feedback from me, adjusting their behaviors, and moving through an activity despite having some struggles. I was then able to introduce more complex activities, such as Build a Vehicle, Stress Ball, and Decorate a Door, and incorporate some more targeted challenges. Whenever the students would enter my room and see some new, exciting item, their eyes would get wide, and I would say, "But what are you expected to do in my room?" In response, they would groan, "Problem solve," and we would have a great time ☺.

Build a Vehicle

SUMMARY

The group will be working together to create a vehicle out of building blocks. Students will be required to follow specific rules, outlined by you, regarding how to participate in the activity. This activity can be as challenging as you want it to be. It only requires two materials and can be repeated several times with small changes made by you. This activity challenges students to work with others on a task they think they understand but that others may have different ideas about.

OBJECTIVE/GOALS

- Students will collaborate and negotiate with others to complete a task.
- Students will demonstrate shared attention and increased awareness of what others are doing.
- Students will be flexible while working with others.

SKILLS SUPPORTED

- Collaboration
- Cooperation
- Emotion Regulation
- Expressive Language
- Flexibility
- Frustration Tolerance
- Impulsivity
- Locus of Control
- Organization
- Planning
- Problem Solving
- Recognizing Nonverbal Cues
- Self-Advocacy
- Self-Regulation
- Shared Attention
- Taking Turns
- Theory of Mind

NUMBER OF STUDENTS

- 1–6

MATERIALS

- LEGO® blocks or other building blocks
- 4" × 4" pieces of paper

PREPARATION

__ Write down random rules students need to follow on small pieces of paper, such as:

You can only use blue pieces (or another specific color).

You cannot use red pieces (or another specific color).

You can only use large pieces.

You can only add a piece after someone adds a blue piece.

You can only use wheels, windows, and axels.

__ Fold the pieces of paper and set them in the middle of the table.

INTRODUCTION

Let the students know they will be building a vehicle together. Do not define what a "vehicle" is. Let the students know that there are some random rules hidden on pieces of paper in the middle of the table and that they each need to select one. Students cannot share their rules with others. As they work on the activity, each student must follow his or her rule and contribute to the overall design and completion of the vehicle.

EXPECTATIONS

Before you begin, review the expectations for the group and emphasize any behaviors you want to see during the session:

- Work together.
- Each person must take a turn before you take your next turn.
- You must follow the rule you select from off the table.
- Do not share your rule with your teammates.

STEPS

1. Ask students to select a piece of folded paper from the center of the table and read the rule to themselves. **This can cause some frustration because the students are excited to build with the blocks and often have a specific idea in their mind as to how they want to do it.** Remind students that they must stick to their rule and that they cannot share their rule with anyone else in the group.

2. Encourage students to decide who should go first. Students will often pick at random or insist that they go first. Sometimes, the first person to start may have a rule that makes it difficult to start building the vehicle (e.g., a rule about only using wheels), which can cause some confusion. This is a great way to start the activity because it forces students to adapt the next time you present the activity; they will think about another way to start that is more purposeful.

3. Have students begin building the vehicle, making sure that they take turns adding blocks to the vehicle. Students likely will not discuss a plan before they begin. Asking the students to do this activity without much direct instruction allows you to repeat this activity again with a discussion on what they learned from the previous experience and how they would like to

tackle the activity based on the challenges they faced and how they think they could do it better.

4. As students build the vehicle, encourage discussion and ask questions about how they think the group should work together. **This activity requires more discussion about the process because much of it highlights what students did *not* do before beginning the task.** You can facilitate a discussion that is very meaningful for what it looks like in the classroom. In addition, students will usually need to be directed to look around and to try to figure out other peoples' rules to successfully work together to build the vehicle. However, let this be a discussion point *after* the first attempt at this activity so that you can see if they adjust their behavior next time.

5. With 10 minutes left, stop the activity and ask students how they are making progress. Then, debrief and reflect on the activity.

CHALLENGES TO INCORPORATE

− Do not say whether students can talk or not.

− Do not define what *vehicle* means before starting.

+ Put very specific rules that will be hard to follow without working with others.

+ Go out of order/turn.

+ Add a piece that does not make sense to the overall design (e.g., a wheel on the top).

+ Accidentally drop the vehicle or break a piece off.

DIFFERENTIATION FOR AGE OR SKILL LEVEL

- **Beginner:** This activity is very difficult for younger children and requires more preparation from you to reduce unnecessary frustrations. If you want to try this activity, it will help to have a LEGO kit or a specific model that the students are working to build, which outlines the specific steps needed to build the vehicle. Have a completed example available—either in picture form or with a model you have made—so students can reference it. You can include rules, but be sure that students will be successful with them; sticking to one color is the easiest rule.

- **Intermediate:** Follow the plan as is, given that this activity is best for middle - or high school-age students.

- **Advanced:** Follow the plan as is, but make the rules more difficult to follow without paying attention to others. For example:

You can only use wheels and windows.

You can only use axels and door frames.

You can only use flat pieces.

These rules force students to look for the person who has a rule that will allow them to add a piece. No one can add a wheel without an axel unless they simply places it on top of another block. Some students will get creative, however ☺.

REFLECTION

The reflection for this activity focuses on increasing students' awareness of thinking ahead, planning, and/or collaborating when working together to complete a task. Ask students what they wish they would have done differently and take notes so you can remind them before they attempt the activity again.

FOLLOW-UP

Wait a week or two and attempt this same activity again to see if students make adjustments. Change the specific rules you had written on the pieces of paper, but outline the activity expectations the same way. The following are other activities that require similar skills:

- Card or Board Games
- Cookie Decorating
- Build a Bridge

GENERALIZATION TO THE CLASSROOM

This activity simulates classroom activities that require students to work in groups and follow directions. It provides an opportunity for students to practice skills when they are not 100% sure of what is expected of them and to be flexible when they have a preconceived idea of how to accomplish a task.

INSTRUCTOR NOTES AND THOUGHTS

_____
_____
_____
_____
_____
_____

LESSON PLAN EXAMPLE: Build a Vehicle

Date: _____3/12_____

Activity: ____Build a Vehicle_____

Students:

_____Todd_____   _____Luke_____

_____Jeremy_____   _____Shawn_____

_____Henry_____   _____

Materials:

☐ LEGO blocks or building blocks

☐ Small pieces of paper

Expectations:

- Work together.
- Each person must take a turn before you take your next turn.
- You must follow the rule you select off the table.
- Do not share your rule with your teammates.
- Have fun!

Steps to Complete:

1. Select a rule off the table.
2. Read your rule silently to yourself. You must follow your rule.
3. Decide who goes first.
4. Be sure each person has a turn before you take your next turn.
5. Build a vehicle.
6. Discuss how you did.

Successes:

- Luke said he was frustrated and did not like the activity, but he participated. He typically shuts down.
- Henry asked for help finding pieces because he felt stuck.

Challenges:

- No one tried to figure out what the other students' rules were. They need to watch each other more.

Next Time:

- Task the group with trying to figure out each other's rule.
- Provide an incentive if they can guess correctly other students' rules by watching what others place on the vehicle.

STUDENT REFLECTION: Build a Vehicle

Date: _____

Activity: _____

Who was here today?

_____   _____

_____   _____

_____   _____

What did you do today?

Today we _____

_____

_____

_____

How did it make you feel?

☐ Satisfied   ☐ Frustrated   ☐ Bored   ☐ _____
☐ Confident   ☐ Irritated   ☐ Sad   ☐ _____
☐ Happy   ☐ Anxious   ☐ Shy   ☐ _____

What did you do well today?

Today I was able to _____

_____

_____

_____

What was the hardest part of the activity?

The hardest part of the activity today was _____

_____

_____

_____

What will you do differently next time?

Next time, I will _____

_____

_____

_____

What happens when you start a task without a plan?

When I start a task without a plan _____

_____

_____

_____

What can you do when you realize you are not sure of how to do something in class?

In class, I will _____

_____

_____

_____

BUILD A VEHICLE

One year, I had an opportunity to work with a small group of students who were identified as gifted and struggled with perfectionism. They experienced intense anxiety about making mistakes and had a difficult time working with classmates in groups; most of them tended to do everything on their own. In talking with their teachers, it was clear that these students would benefit from a brief intervention to support them in developing emotion regulation and social skills. After getting to know each other, I presented them with this activity to see how they could work together to create something that was not clear-cut. The only expectation I added was that they were not allowed to tell anyone their rule. I did not clarify the type of vehicle they were expected to make.

After the students opened their note and read their rule to themselves, one complained, "How am I supposed to do this?" and slammed his note on the table. The students looked around the table with uncertainty, and one student finally said, "I guess I'll go first." His rule only allowed him to use yellow pieces, so he chose a large yellow piece to start the vehicle. The girl next to him could only add small pieces, so she added a single block to the bottom of the yellow piece. She then handed it to the boy next to her, who was the one who had complained earlier. His rule was that he could only add wheels and axles, and he begrudgingly added an axle on to the yellow piece while stating, "This is stupid."

I was the next person to have a turn, and I happened to have gotten the rule to use the largest pieces. I found a large flat plate and asked the students what they thought I should do with it because I thought it would be a good base, but I was not sure if I could rearrange what they had built. One student said, "We don't even know what we are making!" I asked why not, and he replied, "You didn't tell us." I reiterated that we were trying to build a vehicle and that it might be a good idea to have some type of discussion as to what type of vehicle we were trying to make before moving forward. Some students thought we were building an airplane, while others thought we were building a car. We took a brief moment to talk about it and decided to make something like a truck.

Once students came up with the general idea for the vehicle, it started to come together with a little more purpose. It took about three or four passes before they began figuring out each other's rules—and when they did, they began talking more and asking each other for their input. At one point, one student asked, "Can we go out of order?" I replied that I had never said they had to go in any particular order. They all paused with their mouth agape, and one student said, "Oh man! We could have finished this ten minutes ago." After a few more minutes, they were able to finish the activity.

When I presented the activity at a follow-up session, their approach to the task was completely different. They had learned that making assumptions was problematic when working in a group and realized that talking and brainstorming before beginning the task was a good idea so that everyone was on the same page. After they read their rules, they talked together and came up with an idea to build an aircraft. They knew that they could not share their own personal rule, but they became savvy with their questions, asking things like, "Can anyone use a large, flat green piece? Would that person like to go first?" The construction process went much quicker this time.

Through this activity, we had a great discussion about the benefits of working with others during group activities, such as in science lab. Many students shared their frustrations with having to work with others, and they admitted that they often had a hard time recognizing that other people can have different and valuable ideas. In time, we were able to make connections between their experience with the LEGO blocks and their regular classwork, which helped them see the value in collaboration. We finished the session by developing strategies for them to try when working with others, especially those who may have different ideas.

Stress Ball

SUMMARY

Students in the group will each be making a homemade stress ball that they can use whenever they need help in regulating their emotions or focusing their attention. For this activity to be done successfully, students will need to work in pairs, reference a model, plan ahead, and stay patient. This activity can be both fun and frustrating because of the amount of problem solving that is required. As the instructor, you can choose how much modeling and support you provide at the beginning and throughout the activity. In the end, students will have created a tool that reinforces the self-regulation strategies you have already taught.

OBJECTIVE/GOALS

- Students will collaborate with other people to reach a personal goal.
- Students will analyze a problem and come up with a solution.
- Students will make adjustments when things do not go their way.

SKILLS SUPPORTED

- Collaboration
- Cooperation
- Emotion Regulation
- Flexibility
- Following Directions
- Frustration Tolerance
- Impulsivity
- Initiation
- Organization
- Planning
- Problem Solving
- Self-Advocacy
- Self-Regulation
- Sequencing
- Shared Attention
- Taking Turns

NUMBER OF STUDENTS

- 1–6

MATERIALS

- Flour
- Beans
- Rice
- Large balloons (2 per person)
- Latex-free gloves
- Paper
- Tape
- Spoon
- Scissors
- Funnel (optional)

PREPARATION

___ Check for latex allergies (if there is a latex allergy, use socks or latex-free gloves).

___ Purchase the items.

___ Make an example of a stress ball to show students.

___ Create visual with expectations.

___ Create visual with outlined steps.

INTRODUCTION

Students will be making a personal stress ball. Take some time to talk with students about when and why using a stress ball is appropriate and that it is intended to help them think, manage their emotions, and stay on task. Show students the stress ball that you have premade so that they know what they are working toward. Share with students that they will be working with a partner and that they will get to take their stress ball with them at the end of the day.

EXPECTATIONS

Before you begin, review the expectations for the group and emphasize any behaviors you want to see during the session:

- Watch/look at the example.
- Come up with a plan.
- Work with your partner.
- Ask politely.
- Help each other if someone is struggling.
- _____
- _____

STEPS

1. Assign students a partner.
2. Place all the materials in the middle of the table.
3. Show students your final stress ball so they know what they are working toward.
4. Have students choose two balloons that they will use to create their stress ball.
5. Pass around the rice, beans, and flour, and encourage students to hold and feel the items so they can determine which material(s) they want in their stress ball. They can choose to use one type of material or all the materials.
6. Ask each dyad to decide which partner will go first. To create the stress ball, one partner is tasked with holding the balloon open at the top, while the other person fills the balloon with the selected material (e.g., rice, beans, flour, or a combination). Stretching a balloon open can pose challenges for some students because it requires some fine motor strength. Give students an opportunity to try before you intervene. If they are not able to hold it

Stress Ball

open, offer to hold the balloon while they continue to problem solve and make the stress ball.

7. This is the point when you, as the instructor, need to decide whether you will model how to make the stress ball from start to finish. **Often, seeing how the students approach the task first is a good idea given that putting materials inside the balloon is very difficult and requires the use of some type of tool *and* the help of another person.** Every single time I have done this activity, students have tried to put the material in without the use of a funnel. Typically, they will try to place in one single grain of rice or bean at a time or to sprinkle flour in with a spoon, with most of it going on the floor. Most of the time, students will approach the task this way until someone tells them that they will never complete it on time and suggests that they figure out a better way.

8. After giving students some time to approach the task without the use of a funnel, stop the activity and ask the students if the current approach is working.

9. Brainstorm ways people get things into small openings.

10. Show students how to make a funnel out of paper (or present them with a premade funnel), and model how they can use the funnel with their partner to get the material into the balloon.

11. Encourage students to try the task again with the use of a funnel. The amount of material that students put in the balloon will make the stress ball soft or firm. Have students test out the desired firmness of their stress ball, and when they are satisfied, pinch out the air and tie the balloon off.

12. Students will need to cut off the neck of the second balloon and stretch it over the first balloon to complete their stress ball. **This is another step where students will need help from a partner, but wait and see if they ask for help or struggle to get it on by themselves.**

13. When the first student is finished, instruct them to switch roles and follow the same process. Watch to see if they make adjustments during the second try.

14. When all students have completed the task, talk with them about the use of the stress ball and when and where it is appropriate to use. Emphasize that it is not a toy; rather, it is a type of fidget intended to help them self-regulate.

CHALLENGES TO INCORPORATE

Note: This activity is very challenging as is, so you do not necessarily have to insert additional challenges.

– Do not have a funnel available on the table.

– Do not have a solution for how to get materials into the balloon.

– Do not have scissors or tape on the table.

DIFFERENTIATION FOR AGE OR SKILL LEVEL

- **Beginner:** For younger children, it is best to model the entire process at the beginning and include the use of a funnel. Be sure to have steps *explicitly* outlined somewhere visible. An adult may have to be paired with each child, or you can make only one or two stress balls during the session, modeling and supporting one student at a time while the other students observe and give input. Let students know they will each eventually make one to take home. If you are in an educational setting where students are working with a paraprofessional, then this is a good activity for involving the paraprofessional. It provides you with an opportunity to model how to support a child outside of your room, which supports generalization.

- **Intermediate:** Do not have a funnel on the table. Insert suggestions and model solutions as the students work together rather than at the beginning. Volunteer to stretch the balloon open while students fill the balloon. (You may be holding it for a while ☺.) Ask students what they think they could use the piece of paper for.

- **Advanced:** Show the students the finished stress ball and materials, but do not provide any instruction regarding how to make it. Use the first session to see how they brainstorm ways to complete the task and develop a plan that they must all follow at the next session. When they get together to make the stress ball at the second session, make them follow their original plan. Facilitate discussion around how they have to make adjustments once they actually start.

REFLECTION

This activity best highlights problem solving. Reflection for this activity focuses on how to recognize when things become difficult and when to ask for help. As part of the reflection, ask students how they would teach another person how to make a stress ball. This will give you some insight as to how they sequence their thoughts and what they learned from the experience.

FOLLOW-UP

You can make many other types of fidgets with your students using a variety of different materials, such as pipe cleaners, beads, tape, pencils, and craft sticks. Some other fidgets you can make include pencil toppers, weighted beanbags, nuts-and-bolts sticks, gel sensory bags, and an ocean in a bottle. Look up how to make homemade fidgets and get creative. The *process* is what you are going for here; the product is an added bonus for children to use and apply their skills. Other activities that require similar skills include the following:

- Snow Globe
- Peanut Butter & Jelly
- Build a Vehicle
- Build a Bridge

GENERALIZATION TO THE CLASSROOM

This activity simulates classroom activities where students have to work together with others to create a product. It also forces them to stop and think when something is not going as planned rather than forcing a solution or giving up. It is one of the best activities for helping students know when they should take a break or ask for help.

INSTRUCTOR NOTES AND THOUGHTS

LESSON PLAN EXAMPLE: Stress Ball

Date: _____02/02_____

Activity: ____Stress Ball_____

Students:

_____Nick_____   _____Carlos_____

_____Rita_____   _____

_____Jesse_____   _____

Materials:

- ☐ Dry beans
- ☐ Flour
- ☐ Rice
- ☐ Balloons (2 per person)
- ☐ Paper
- ☐ Scissors
- ☐ Tape
- ☐ Funnel (optional)

Expectations:

- Look at the example.
- Come up with a plan.
- Work with your partner.
- Ask politely.
- Take a break if you need one.
- Help each other.

Steps to Complete:

1. Choose two balloons.
2. Choose the material(s) you want in your balloon.
3. Pick which partner goes first.
4. Hold open the first balloon while your partner fills it with material.
5. Tie off the first balloon.
6. Cut off the top of the second balloon.
7. Stretch the second balloon over the top of the first balloon.
8. Switch and help your partner create their stress ball.

Successes:
- Nick figured out that he needed a funnel to get the rice into his balloon, and he asked how to make one.
- Jesse was very patient when the flour spilled on the floor, and he asked for help to clean it up.

Challenges:
- Rita tried to put one bean in at a time for 5 minutes and did not look around to see what others were doing.

Next Time:
- Ask students to verbalize their plan before they start so they can listen to different ideas.

STUDENT REFLECTION: Stress Ball

Date: _____

Activity: _____

Who was here today?

_____   _____
_____   _____
_____   _____

What did you do today?

Today we _____
_____
_____
_____

How did it make you feel?

☐ Satisfied	☐ Frustrated	☐ Bored	☐ _____
☐ Confident	☐ Irritated	☐ Sad	☐ _____
☐ Happy	☐ Anxious	☐ Shy	☐ _____

What did you do well today?

Today I was able to _____
_____
_____
_____

What was the hardest part of the activity?

The hardest part of the activity today was _____
_____
_____
_____
_____

What do you usually do when something gets really hard?

When things are hard for me, I usually _____

_____

_____

How can you tell it is time to take a break from something?

I know I need to take a break when I _____

_____

_____

How can you tell someone else is getting frustrated?

I can tell someone is getting frustrated when _____

_____

_____

What will you do differently next time?

Next time, I will _____

_____

_____

How would you explain to someone else how to do this activity?

If I were to teach someone else how to make their own stress ball, I would first _____

_____

Then, I would _____

_____

These are the steps I would tell them to follow:

1. _____
2. _____
3. _____
4. _____
5. _____
6. _____

Case Example: STRESS BALL

Sydney was a seventh-grade student diagnosed with autism spectrum disorder. She was often observed reading books in class when she was not directly prompted to do schoolwork, and she often appeared disconnected from her surroundings. When she participated in class, she made off-topic comments and blurted her thoughts out at inopportune times. She participated in a small social skills group every week, and I struggled to get her to pay attention to the other students and what they were doing. When Christie and I presented the stress ball activity to the group, Sydney was excited to make one and appeared attentive as we modeled the directions—or so we thought.

We had six students in the group and put them into pairs. Sydney was paired with a boy who was very shy, and not saying much, he sat next to her as the other four students immediately got started. Sydney took a balloon and the bag of rice, and she set it in front of herself as her partner sat quietly watching her. She then proceeded to drop one single grain of rice into the balloon opening at a time. Sydney's partner and I watched her attempt to fill her balloon in this manner for about 5 minutes. I told her that we only had 30 minutes to complete the activity and that she was not going to get it done on time using her current method, but she never looked up or acknowledged me as she continued.

Eventually, I had to be more direct with Sydney, and I instructed her to work with her partner by directing him to hold the balloon open while she filled it with rice. She agreed and handed him the balloon. Because he was trying to stretch it open, she attempted to put a handful of rice into the balloon, which resulted in about 90% of it falling on the floor. When I told her that she needed to have her balloon filled with rice in the next 3 minutes, she still did not appear to listen to me. Her partner said, "Sydney, can we use a funnel?" She paused for a moment and looked up at him. He pointed out that the team next to them was using a funnel and that they were making much faster progress. She immediately looked over at the other students and asked, "Can I have one of those?" I had an extra funnel and handed it to her. She and her partner then worked together to stretch the balloon over the funnel, and she even said to him directly, "Hold it tight so it doesn't fall out."

Although Sydney and her partner only finished one stress ball together during that session, it was a huge success. The activity forced her to look up and see what others were doing—and it happened because another student asked her to. It also forced a student, who otherwise kept quiet and allowed other people to do things for him, to give a suggestion. I had to be patient and allow Sydney's partner to become uncomfortable so that he had an opportunity to speak up and intervene. I have always found that when students give instructions or ideas to other students, they are much more receptive and responsive.

Scavenger Hunt

SUMMARY

This activity encourages students to interact with others outside of your room and think from another person's perspective. This activity gives you an opportunity to help clients learn about navigating their environment and approaching people to ask for information. It is an excellent activity to do when students are transitioning into a new environment or school. It is one way to help them learn their way around the building and to find the resources they will need access to. You can get very creative with fun things your students need to find, or (if you have the skills) you can create riddles that they need to figure out. Students do not necessarily have to move from place to place for this activity to be effective, but it is a lot more fun.

OBJECTIVE/GOALS

- Students will interpret double meanings, nonliteral language, and/or vague descriptions.
- Students will negotiate and collaborate to meet a goal.
- Students will recognize when they need to ask for help.

SKILLS SUPPORTED

- Cooperation
- Expressive (and Receptive) Language
- Flexibility
- Following Directions
- Impulsivity
- Life Skills
- Listening
- Planning
- Problem Solving
- Recognizing Nonverbal Cues
- Self-Advocacy
- Shared Attention
- Taking Turns
- Theory of Mind

NUMBER OF STUDENTS

- 1–6

MATERIALS

- Notecards
- Pen
- Snack of your choosing
- Map (optional)

PREPARATION

__ Create note cards with clues, or use the "Sample Scavenger Hunt" sheet (p. 104).

__ Talk with any other adults who may be helping with the scavenger hunt (e.g., people who will be asked for items).

__ Place items in areas that the scavenger hunt directs the students to.

__ Have some type of treat at the very end (treasure ☺).

__ Check for allergies.

INTRODUCTION

Let students know that they will be doing a scavenger hunt today. Ask if anyone knows what a scavenger hunt is. Then, explain that they will be given a sheet of paper with a list of items that they need to collect as a team. Explain that some items will be easy to find, while others will require them to approach people and ask for something. When students have checked off all the items on their list, they can come back to the room and share a treat.

EXPECTATIONS

Before you begin, review the expectations for the group and emphasize any behaviors you want to see during the session:

- Look through your list and come up with a plan for how to get all the items.
- Take turns reading clues or finding items.
- Ask politely.
- Ask clarifying questions (you will need to practice what this looks like).
- _____
- _____

STEPS

1. Before you start, decide how much time students will be given to complete the scavenger hunt and tell them before they begin. Limiting it to 20 to 25 minutes works well so you have some time to debrief. If they do not finish it during the first session, you can complete it next time.

2. Pass out the "Sample Scavenger Hunt" sheet or the note cards that you created with clues.

3. Review the items with students, and ask students which items they think will be the most difficult to find.

4. Decide which students will be responsible for checking off which items. Allow students to negotiate why they want certain items so they can compromise and come to a fair conclusion. You may need to intervene if one student takes over.

5. Brainstorm ways to get the difficult items. Ask questions such as "Who do you think you should ask?" or "Where would we find something like that?"

6. Practice ways to appropriately ask others for items. Students can get excited and stressed about needing to check off items on their list. When students become too eager or stressed,

they tend to interrupt others, approach people at inopportune times, and ask for items very bluntly. If students need to approach a person to collect an item, practice how to approach the person and what to say; creating a note card that they can refer to when they are in the situation sets them up for success. Sometimes, students also need to learn to build context into how they approach someone. For this activity, they will need to be taught to say, "We are doing a scavenger hunt. Do you have . . ."

7. Given the time required for this activity, your assigning who goes first is generally best. From there, the students can negotiate which task should be tackled next. Some items might be close in proximity, and it will be more efficient to decide items based on location. However, most students will attempt to go through the list in order and will often not finish in time because of it. This gives you a great opportunity to talk about how to tackle multistep tasks and to encourage them to look at all the things they need to complete before beginning. You can also talk about the importance of developing a plan and creating a mental map before beginning. When you do this activity again, see if they make adjustments. If they do not, remind them before they leave your room that they need to create a plan to be more efficient.

8. Start the scavenger hunt. As students move through the building, hang back and take some notes as you observe their behaviors. This activity provides you with an excellent example of how they behave outside of your room and problem solve in unstructured environments. If students become frustrated or overwhelmed, offer a simple suggestion or, if needed, to take a brief break to your room. This is a great opportunity to directly teach when it is a good time to remove yourself from a situation and compose yourself before plowing through something just to get it done.

9. When time is up, or all the items have been checked off, go back to your room and share the treat ("treasure"). Oreos® are often a group favorite, but check for allergies. If you have written clues or riddles, be sure that the last one guides them back to your room. If you have made the hunt very difficult and they are unable finish, enforce the predetermined time limit and go back to the room for the treat. There are times when students have to learn that "enough is enough." Talk about how and why they can make that decision, as well as when it is appropriate. This also provides you with an opportunity to talk about advocating for themselves when things become too difficult.

10. As you share the treat, talk about what went well and ask students what was hard about the scavenger hunt.

CHALLENGES TO INCORPORATE

– Act like you do not know how to find anything.

+ Make an absurd suggestion as to where you think students could get an item.

+ Do not allow the students to talk during the hunt; require them to gesture or write instead.

+ Encourage one of the people the students approach to not have the item and to, instead, give a suggestion for where students might be able to find it.

DIFFERENTIATION FOR AGE OR SKILL LEVEL

- **Beginner:** Create a simple list of items that are very literal and direct. This activity provides you with an opportunity to work on vocabulary skills. Consult with parents, teachers, and the school's speech-language pathologist to know which vocabulary words will support the students' learning.

- **Intermediate:** Incorporate more items that require students to interact with other people. You can also create a list that has a loose description of items, which requires students to be more purposeful when planning where to get an item.
- **Advanced:** Add items to your scavenger hunt that are basically impossible to find and see how students problem solve. Ultimately, in life, there are times when you cannot accomplish something 100%, but you need to be able to make decisions and have a strong rationale for why something could not be completed. The following statements are not adequate: "It's not fair," "But I didn't know how," or "The dog ate it." If you want to get very creative, you can create clues where students have to solve a riddle to find the next clue. A lot of examples are online, and watching students work together can be really fun.

REFLECTION

Reflection for this activity focuses on the skills that students need to successfully navigate their environment, particularly when it is an environment that they are unfamiliar with. Sometimes, students overestimate what they are capable of doing and do not ask for help. Reflection for this activity also provides you an opportunity to discuss how students can recognize who they should approach and where they should go when they are in an unfamiliar situation.

FOLLOW-UP

Make a small scavenger hunt *with* the students. This will give them an opportunity to come up with clues and think about how the reader will conceptualize what is written on the clue in order to interpret it correctly. Often, students will write a clue that is very literal and direct (e.g., "Go to the gym"), and you will have to provide support as to how they can expand their language to allude to the clue rather than being so direct. This helps students create mental maps and think of ways that they can communicate directions to other people in a clear and concise manner. You can also play the game, Mind Trap, which involves a large set of cards with word puzzles and riddles that can be done in your office. The game requires students to ask clarifying questions and consider double meanings, and it leads to excellent discussions. Other activities that require similar skills include the following:

- Back-to-Back Drawing
- Peanut Butter & Jelly
- Build a Vehicle

GENERALIZATION TO THE CLASSROOM

This activity gives the students opportunities to practice approaching other people and asking for information. This skill is necessary whenever they are in a new environment and do not know how to find something, such as a bathroom. This activity ultimately supports students' ability to ask questions with confidence and to advocate for themselves.

INSTRUCTOR NOTES AND THOUGHTS

Sample Scavenger Hunt #1

Find each item on the list and check it off:

- ☐ Find a blue pen.
- ☐ What time is it? _____
- ☐ Find a person with a calendar and ask him or her what day of the week Mother's Day falls on. Write the date here: _____
- ☐ Ask someone for directions to the nearest bathroom.
- ☐ Find something green that you can hold with both hands.
- ☐ Look up the fourth word in the dictionary.
- ☐ Find someone with a summer birthday and get their signature on the following line:

  _____

Sample Scavenger Hunt #2

Find each item on the list and check it off:

- ☐ How many bathrooms are in the building? _____
- ☐ Go to the place you might learn how to play basketball.
- ☐ Where can you sit for lunch? _____
- ☐ Find a book written by a female author.
- ☐ If you lose something, you might find it here: _____
- ☐ Find the person who knows the building the best and ask them what time school gets out: _____

LESSON PLAN EXAMPLE: Scavenger Hunt

Date: _____10/10_____

Activity: ____Scavenger Hunt____

Students:

_____Sarah_____   _____

_____Cade_____   _____

_____Noah_____   _____

Materials:

☐ Scavenger hunt sheet

☐ Pen

Expectations:

- Read through the scavenger hunt list before you start.
- Develop a plan together for how to collect all the items.
- Ask politely.
- Ask clarifying questions.
- Be patient.
- Have fun!

Steps to Complete:

1. Read through the scavenger hunt list.
2. Brainstorm places to collect the items.
3. Decide which person will be responsible for which items.
4. Begin your hunt.
5. Finish hunt.
6. Share a treat.

Successes:

- Cade was confident when approaching someone in the hall to ask for directions to the nearest bathroom.

Challenges:

- Noah became very frustrated when he was tasked with asking someone for a marker because he knew that there was one in my office. He argued that he did not have to ask someone for one.
- The group did not really work together. They took responsibility for their individual items but did not support one another much.

Next Time:

- We will play riddle games so students have to think a bit more and talk together.
- Or we will do another scavenger hunt but not allow the students to talk.

STUDENT REFLECTION: Scavenger Hunt

Date: _____

Activity: _____

Who was here today?

_____   _____

_____   _____

_____   _____

What did you do today?

Today we _____

_____

_____

_____

How did it make you feel?

☐ Satisfied	☐ Frustrated	☐ Bored	☐ _____
☐ Confident	☐ Irritated	☐ Sad	☐ _____
☐ Happy	☐ Anxious	☐ Shy	☐ _____

What did you do well today?

Today I was able to _____

_____

_____

_____

What was the hardest part of the activity?

The hardest part of the activity today was _____

_____

_____

_____

What can you do if you are in a new environment?

When I am in an unfamiliar place, I can _____

_____

_____

_____

How can you tell if someone might be helpful?

I can tell someone might help me when _____

_____

_____

_____

Have you ever been to a new place?   Yes   No

What is it like when you are in a new place and do not know where to go?

When I am in a new place and am not sure where to go, I _____

_____

_____

_____

What can you do in class when you are not sure how to do something?

In class, I can _____

_____

_____

_____

What will you do differently next time?

Next time, I will _____

_____

_____

_____

SCAVENGER HUNT

This activity first came together when I was helping transition a group of eighth graders into high school. Many students were excited to start a new school, but they were concerned or worried about several things. Many of their parents also expressed concerns about the size of the school and whether their child would adjust quickly to maneuvering through the school and between classes. The resource teacher and I had initially planned two tours of the high school so students could meet their new resource teachers and get a feel for the building. However, what we quickly learned was that the students followed us around somewhat aimlessly and did not appear to be paying attention. In turn, I requested one more tour of the high school and asked the high school service providers to collaborate with me in creating a scavenger hunt to ensure that the students were more engaged while exploring their new environment.

When I took six students to the high school for the third time, there was some griping because they felt they already knew what to expect and did not need to go again. However, I knew that they were also anxious because they stuck close together and avoided looking at the high school students as we made our way down to the resource room. When we got there, I introduced them to the school's social worker and psychologist, and I let them know that we were going to be completing a scavenger hunt to help them better learn the high school environment and feel prepared when they came back in the fall. The students rolled their eyes and folded their arms, but they perked up when I told them that they could have Twizzlers® and Oreos if they checked off all the items on the list.

For this scavenger hunt, we made sure that the items to be checked off were all basic, obvious places that they needed to familiarize themselves with so they could easily find an adult for help or orient themselves if they got lost: the resource room, gymnasium, cafeteria, front office, library, counseling office, and each wing in the high school. I prioritized requiring an interaction with a person at each destination so that the students could practice approaching an adult in the building, asking a question, and getting their needs met (e.g., "Go to the counseling office, find the ninth-grade counselor, and ask to borrow a blue pen").

I passed out the list of places to check off and separated the students into two groups of three. I told them that if they got lost or needed help, they could always ask an adult or come back to the resource room to regroup. One student commented, "We are going to look weird." I told her that scavenger hunts are something that most people know about, and if she wanted to, she could start her question or conversation with "We are doing a scavenger hunt, and I am supposed to ask a counselor for a blue pen. Do you have one I can borrow?" She seemed okay with the suggestion and looked back at the list.

I gave the students about five minutes to look over their list and encouraged them to write the name of the person who was responsible for each task next to the box so they could be prepared, and I then sent them on their way. As the students worked their way through the building, I followed behind, doing my best to not be seen, so that I could follow up with the adults they interacted with. Everyone shared that they were very respectful and did a great job.

Nothing about this scavenger hunt was overly complicated or exciting, but it did provide the students with a concrete opportunity to actively learn about their new environment and practice approaching people with the support of a familiar adult (e.g., me) so that they had some experience to rely on in the fall. Their behavior and level of engagement during this third tour differed drastically from the first two tours, and I really felt that they took more ownership for being there. When we got back to my office, we shared some Oreos and Twizzlers, and I asked them what they were looking forward to in high school again. This time, they appeared a little less nervous and talked about being able to have whatever they wanted for lunch.

Build a Bridge

SUMMARY

For this activity, the group will be working together to build a bridge or structure that will be able to hold something off the ground. This task should be completely novel to the kids, so they will have to think creatively, work together, remain patient, and adjust their strategy.

OBJECTIVE/GOALS

- Students will collaborate and listen to others.
- Students will demonstrate flexibility and make adjustments.
- Students will identify factors/circumstances that cause frustration and stress.

SKILLS SUPPORTED

- Collaboration
- Cooperation
- Emotion Regulation
- Flexibility
- Following Directions
- Frustration Tolerance
- Initiation
- Listening
- Locus of Control
- Organization
- Planning
- Problem Solving
- Self-Advocacy
- Self-Regulation
- Sequencing
- Shared Attention
- Taking Turns
- Theory of Mind

NUMBER OF STUDENTS

- 1–6

MATERIALS

- White Paper
- Newspaper
- Masking tape
- Stapler
- Markers

PREPARATION

__ Collect a lot of newspaper or ask others to bring some in.

__ Create visual with expectations.

__ Create visual with outlined steps.

INTRODUCTION

Together, students will be building a bridge that will hold something off the ground. They will have to make the structure using only paper, tape, and staples—and they will need to ensure that the structure is sturdy. The bridge has to stand on its own, without anyone touching or supporting it, and has to hold some weight. When students are finished, they will test the bridge to see how much weight it will hold.

EXPECTATIONS

Before you begin, review the expectations for the group and emphasize any behaviors you want to see during the session:

- Listen to each other's ideas.
- Brainstorm ideas together.
- Be patient.
- Be flexible.
- If you want to make a change, let the group know.
- Share materials.
- _____
- _____

STEPS

Session 1: Brainstorm

1. Spread out the building materials on the floor so students can examine them.

2. Discuss how students can use these materials to make a bridge. For example, ask students how they can make newspaper sturdy when it is so flimsy.

3. Instruct each student to design a bridge on a piece of paper. **Students may need some recommendations regarding the design so that they do not try to make it overly complex.** I have seen a student try to make the Golden Gate Bridge, which will never get done on time. The designs should be fairly simple because students will not actually know what works until they start constructing it. The draft of the bridge will end up being drastically different from the final product because they will make a lot of adjustments as they go along.

4. Require each student to present his or her idea to the group, and have a discussion about which ideas or designs should be incorporated into the final bridge idea.

5. Design a draft to start building at the next session, and make a rough sketch of the bridge design on a piece of paper.

Sessions 2 and 3: Start Construction

1. Post the previous design you came up with on the wall so students can refer to it when building the bridge. **In contrast to the Teacher Appreciation Cards and Decorating a Door activities, students will not be required to follow this draft.** They will have to constantly make changes and adjustments as they begin construction. This is a completely novel task, and students will be experimenting to see how they can make newspaper and tape into something sturdy.

2. Give each student some newspaper and tape, and encourage them to practice manipulating the items to see how they can make it sturdy. Observe how they are approaching the task. Most kids will try to fold paper multiple times or scrunch it to make it thick. **Rolling the newspaper is the best way to make it have structure.** The tighter you roll it, the stronger it will be. If you are an active participant, you can model some ways to build the structure without telling them. See if the students look around and adjust their approach based on what they notice. If they are not looking around, comment, "Hey, this seems to work!"

3. Once students have had practice with some newspaper and tape, encourage them to make sections of the bridge so they can put it all together. As students complete each section of the bridge, set each section aside until all the pieces are complete.

4. When students feel that they have enough sections, begin putting them all together. As the facilitator, step back during this time to observe how the students interact and attempt to create a structure. **The final bridge may or may not resemble the initial draft, and that is a reflection of being flexible and problem solving in the moment.**

Final Session: Test It Out

1. Place the finished bridge on the floor or table, and step back.

2. Carefully start adding weight to the bridge to see how strong the students have made it. You can add single items that have different weights, or you can pile on several of the same item one at a time. Some items to consider are paper clips, pencils, a pad of paper, and a book.

3. Continue adding weight until the bridge collapses.

4. Clean up.

5. Once students have tested their bridge, talk with them about the process and where they can make adjustments to make the bridge stronger.

6. Repeat this activity in a few weeks or months to see if they make these adjustments and change their approach.

CHALLENGES TO INCORPORATE

Note: This activity is challenging as is because it requires students to experiment and make changes in the moment.

– Provide less support with brainstorming.

+ Start building on your own bridge.

DIFFERENTIATION FOR AGE OR SKILL LEVEL

- **Beginner:** Create a simple design ahead of time and ask the students to use the materials to make the bridge you designed. Making a bridge with four legs and a top is simple. Making it sturdy is the hard part. Or prepare individual bridge pieces ahead of time and require students to come up with the best way to assemble the pieces into a structure that can hold weight.
- **Intermediate:** The outline for the activity is appropriate as is. Be a participant and provide suggestions (and/or model) in the moment to help students make adjustments.
- **Advanced:** Break the group into two smaller groups and have them compete to see which team can build the strongest bridge. Or establish the expectation that the bridge will be required to hold at least two to three large books.

REFLECTION

Reflection for this activity focuses on preplanning and being flexible when your plan cannot be carried out as expected.

FOLLOW-UP

Repeat this activity in a few weeks or months and add some different materials, like straws or sticks. You can also look up various simple STEM (science, technology, engineering, and mathematics) activities online with the group and ask them what they would like to try next. Other activities that require similar skills include the following:

- Stress Ball
- Decorate a Door
- Back-to-Back Drawing
- Plan a Party

GENERALIZATION TO THE CLASSROOM

This activity emulates classroom activities where students have to be creative, flexible, and make adjustments based on circumstances and materials. Much like STEM activities, students have to use the materials they have on hand to make something functional. It is also similar to any situation in which individuals have to make adjustments in the moment, which can involve a schedule change or an unexpected transition.

INSTRUCTOR NOTES AND THOUGHTS

_____
_____
_____
_____
_____

LESSON PLAN EXAMPLE: Build a Bridge

Date: _____04/12_____

Activity: _____Build a Bridge_____

Students:

_____Seth_____	_____Natasha_____
_____Beckett_____	_____Brandy_____
_____Julio_____	_____Conner_____

Materials:

- ☐ White paper
- ☐ Newspaper
- ☐ Tape
- ☐ Staples
- ☐ Markers

Expectations:

- Listen to each other's ideas.
- Brainstorm ideas together.
- Be patient.
- Be flexible.
- If you want to make a change, let the group know.
- Share materials.

Steps to Complete:

1. Listen to directions.
2. Look at materials.
3. Brainstorm ideas.
4. Draw a bridge design.
5. Decide on a design for the group.
6. Practice using the paper and tape.
7. Build individual pieces of the bridge.
8. Assemble the bridge.
9. Test its strength.

Successes:
- Brandy asked the other kids what their ideas were.
- Julio started rolling papers and asked Beckett to help him tape.

Challenges:
- Conner folded his arms and refused to participate.

Next Time:
- Give Conner a job (e.g., passing out tape and paper) so he knows exactly what he can do.

STUDENT REFLECTION: Build a Bridge

Date: _____

Activity: _____

Who was here today?

_____   _____
_____   _____
_____   _____

What did you do today?

Today we _____

_____

_____

_____

How did it make you feel?

☐ Satisfied	☐ Frustrated	☐ Bored	☐ _____
☐ Confident	☐ Irritated	☐ Sad	☐ _____
☐ Happy	☐ Anxious	☐ Shy	☐ _____

What did you do well today?

Today I was able to _____

_____

_____

_____

What was the hardest part of the activity?

The hardest part of the activity today was _____

_____

_____

_____

What will you do differently next time?

Next time, I will _____

_____

_____

_____

When is it a good idea to adjust your plan or make changes to your plan?

Sometimes, I have to make changes to my plan because _____

_____

_____

_____

When are there times when you have to be flexible?

I have to be flexible when _____

_____

_____

_____

 # BUILD A BRIDGE

One year, a high school resource teacher and I presented this activity with a small class of about eight students; half were students I worked with directly, and the other half had IEPs to support their learning. I had initially talked with the resource teacher about completing this activity in my small group, but she suggested we do it together during her math period because the whole class was struggling with impulsivity, organization, planning, and group work. We thought the activity would be a great "team building" exercise that would also highlight the drawbacks of rushing through work. It would also allow students to generalize skills they had learned in my small group to the exact environment where they needed to apply them.

We decided to break the class into two teams of four and presented the activity as a competition to see which group could build the strongest bridge out of newspaper and tape. We split the activity into two parts, the first being a brainstorming session with some newspaper and tape they could experiment with and the second being the bridge building competition itself. I took one group into my office and presented them with a large stack of newspaper and tape, and I told them they had the entire period to practice with the materials and come up with a design for the following week.

When we got to the room, the students immediately began talking about what they thought the structure should look like and how big it should be. I had to slow them down and suggest that they start sharing their ideas one at a time. One student had a hard time verbally describing his idea and asked to draw it on a piece of paper, which led to *all* the students drawing their design on a piece of paper, some of which included far too much detail. Given that the group was spending too much time trying to come up with the perfect design on paper, I encouraged them to instead work with the newspaper and tape itself to show each other their ideas. One kid began to scrunch up pieces of newspaper into balls and tape them together. Another student started rolling up large tubes and suggested that they use them for legs.

Students quickly learned that they could not get the newspaper to reflect the complicated designs they had drawn on paper. One student said, "Newspaper is too thin. There is no way this is going to hold something! It keeps collapsing." The student who rolled the newspaper said, "Hey, look, this seems strong." Another said, "Let's just roll it all up, and then we can figure how to make the top later." At this point, they did not attempt any other strategies, and they all began rolling newspaper into tubes, with some being very thick and tall, and others being thin and short. What started out as four individuals having their own ideas ended up as four students holding pieces of rolled-up newspaper for each other while trying different ways to construct the bridge. It was the most collaboration I had seen from them, and I did not have to intervene or provide support.

After experimenting with ways to make the newspaper stronger, the team ended up drafting a fairly simple bridge—a wide base with four legs that were rolled up like pillars and several long pieces that were rolled up and taped together at the top. It looked more like a table than a bridge, but we never put any restrictions or explicitly defined what a bridge was other than it had to hold some weight and keep things off the ground.

Going into the competition, we were pretty confident as a team. Although my team members stuck with their original design, they rushed through the construction stage and began frantically rolling newspaper and taping it together. The resulting bridge was able to stand on its own, but many tubes were weak because students did not place enough emphasis on firmly rolling the pieces together. The other team appeared more composed and methodical; they had a checklist and assigned each student to a role (e.g., rollers, tapers, and holders). The other team actually ended up designing a very similar bridge, but their structured process made for a much more stable base than ours. I teased the resource teacher about providing more guidance and structure to her team than I did.

When time was up, we began testing the strength of each bridge by putting small items, such as pencils and pads of paper, on top. Both bridges were able to withstand this lighter load, so we then decided to test which bridge could hold the most textbooks. Our team was able to carry the weight of two full textbooks before the legs collapsed, and the second team was able to add six before their bridge folded over on itself. One student on my team commented, "That's not fair; we had basically the same thing!"

The resource teacher and I then had a brief discussion about what they thought the differences were between the two bridges. One student finally said, "The other team was careful, and we just threw ours together because we were afraid we wouldn't get it done in time. We should have rolled the tubes tighter. Then we would have won." We spent the next period reflecting on the activity and connecting what we observed during the bridge-building process to how the students typically behaved and performed in class. We highlighted that we often observed them impulsively beginning tasks without first thinking through a plan, rushing through their work, and then becoming upset with the outcome.

Overall, students had fun with this activity, and for the remainder of the semester, the resource teacher reported that the entire class seemed to enjoy being together more, which greatly facilitated group work. Additionally, the students I worked with directly gained a clearer understanding of how the skills we practiced in small group transferred to larger settings. I was subsequently able to support them by introducing more focused activities that required them to methodically develop a plan and stick to it to complete a task well.

Cookie Decorating

SUMMARY

The group will be decorating cookies to eat and will be required to demonstrate flexibility in doing so. This activity is one of the more challenging activities and should be presented only after you have completed several other activities. Although this activity can be completed in one session, it is broken down into two separate parts. As the instructor, make sure to participate and model throughout.

OBJECTIVE/GOALS

- Students will demonstrate flexibility.
- Students will identify factors/circumstances that cause frustration and stress.
- Students will advocate for their needs.

SKILLS SUPPORTED

- Collaboration
- Cooperation
- Emotion Regulation
- Flexibility
- Following Directions
- Frustration Tolerance
- Impulsivity
- Initiation
- Life Skills
- Expressive Language
- Listening
- Locus of Control
- Organization
- Planning
- Problem Solving
- Self-Advocacy
- Self-Regulation
- Sequencing
- Shared Attention
- Taking Turns
- Theory of Mind

NUMBER OF STUDENTS

- 1–8

Note: The activity can be done with fewer students, but its complexity is what makes it a good activity to see if students are generalizing skills.

MATERIALS

- Store-bought sugar cookies
- Tub of white frosting
- Colored icing for decorating
- Sprinkles
- 2–3 types of candy
- Paper
- Colored pencils
- Napkins
- Knives

PREPARATION

__ Check for allergies.

__ Purchase the cookie items.

__ Make a sample cookie design on a piece of paper (see "Sample Cookie Design" on page 127).

__ Outline steps and expectations before students arrive.

__ Place items in the middle of the table.

INTRODUCTION

Students will be designing and decorating cookies. Encourage students to look at all the items on the table so they can have an idea of what they would like to put on their cookie. Share with students that they will first design how they want to decorate their cookie on a piece of paper and that they will be asked to decorate a cookie to match the design they have in front of them. When students have decorated their cookie, they will be asked to show the group the decorated cookie to compare it to the paper design before eating it.

EXPECTATIONS

Before you begin, review the expectations for the group and emphasize any behaviors you want to see during the session:

- Wash your hands first.
- Wait your turn.
- Look at the toppings on the table and consider them before you begin your design.
- Share and ask politely.
- Follow your cookie design exactly.
- Wait until everyone is finished before you eat your cookie.
- Have fun!
- _____
- _____

Cookie Decorating 123

STEPS

This is an activity that you can do more than once so you can see how students adjust their behaviors. Only post one portion of steps at a time. Part 2 can be posted while students are washing their hands.

Part 1

1. Share with students that they will be decorating cookies but that they have to design their decoration before they can begin.
2. Ask one student to pass out pieces of paper with a circle already drawn on it (make a copy of the "Cookie Design Template" on page 126), and let them know that it represents their cookie.
3. Place all the cookie-decorating materials in the middle of the table so that students can see what is available.
4. Encourage students to look at the materials on the table before they begin drawing, and let them know that they can use any of the materials to decorate their cookie.
5. Show students how to design their cookie by modeling looking around the table, talking through your process aloud, and roughly drawing what you would like to put on your cookie.
6. When you model drawing your cookie design for students, make sure to clearly label the different toppings you include on your design (e.g., placement of frosting, placement of candy and sprinkles, specific colors, etc.). See the "Sample Cookie Design" on page 127 as an example.
7. Give students approximately five minutes to design their cookie on the piece of paper, and provide several prompts for how much time is left.
8. When each student is finished, collect the designs and instruct students to go wash their hands.

Part 2

1. When students return from washing their hands, pass out one cookie to each student on a napkin.
2. Redistribute the paper designs *randomly*, making sure they do not get the design they created.
3. Instruct the students to decorate the cookie they have in front of them. **This is typically the part of the activity in which students become the most frustrated and upset and when they will need the most support.** You may need to encourage them to be flexible and help them problem solve so that they can participate in the activity. Having extra cookies in case it is a big problem and allowing them to have a plain one once they have attempted the activity are helpful.
4. Encourage students to ask politely for the ingredients they need and to share the decorating materials.
5. Allow the students to decorate their cookie. **Most students will begin decorating the cookie and never ask the original artist clarifying questions. This is the time when you decide how much more instruction and support you provide.** You need to decide if you want students to be required to collaborate and ask questions or if you want to see

what happens naturally the first time and debrief at the end about how students could have done it differently.

6. Make the students wait until all the cookies have been completed.

7. Before students can eat their cookie, go around the table and ask each student to present their cookie while another student holds up the picture to compare how the actual cookie looks to the picture. **You can decide whether students are allowed to comment on each other's cookie design.** Some students can become defensive if others say the cookie does not look like the picture. However, for older students, this provides an opportunity to handle feelings of conflict or insult.

8. Ask each student to share whether the activity was difficult and, if so, how. Often, the designer did not label or was not specific enough in the instructions and design. Other times, there is too much detail to reasonably get the entire design onto one cookie. Discussions about difficulties such as these are encouraged so that students can practice getting feedback and providing thoughts about their process as well.

9. Eat cookies!

10. If there is time, you can reflect on how the overall process went once students have eaten their cookies, or during the next session. Attempting this activity again later in the semester to see what students do to make the cookie look more like the paper design is a good idea.

CHALLENGES TO INCORPORATE

Note: This project is challenging as is, with the biggest challenge being the redistribution of designs. If you think redistributing the designs is too much, you can have students follow their own direction first.

– Only have one or two knives available.

– Place the cookies out of reach.

+ Ask for all the red candies and be adamant about it.

+ Mess up the cookie design.

+ Try to put your finger in the icing.

+ Do not share a candy.

DIFFERENTIATION FOR AGE OR SKILL LEVEL

- **Beginner:** Have students follow their own design instead of randomly redistributing the designs. Do the steps together one at a time, and encourage students to label the toppings they are putting on their paper design. Reflect on how following directions is easier when they are written clearly.

- **Intermediate:** Follow the steps as outlined. If the students are struggling, provide additional supports for how to ask clarifying questions.

- **Advanced:** Do not intervene with problem solving. Be annoying and see how students respond to your not sharing or making an overly complex design.

REFLECTION

This activity is more complex, providing students with several challenges. Reflection for this activity can focus on any particular thing that tripped up the students. Discussions can also focus on what to do and how to handle yourself when something unexpected happens.

FOLLOW-UP

Complete a reflection write-up during the next session. Do this activity again in a month or so and do not provide extra instruction, or encourage students to invite a friend. You can also play a card game with made-up instructions. Other activities that require similar skills include the following:

- Card or Board Games
- Build a Vehicle
- Back-to-Back Drawing
- Stress Ball

GENERALIZATION TO THE CLASSROOM

This activity simulates classroom activities in which students have to plan ahead, create a rough draft, and complete a project that is similar to what they planned in the first place. It also simulates scenarios in which directions or expectations change and students are expected to demonstrate flexibility.

INSTRUCTOR NOTES AND THOUGHTS

_____
_____
_____
_____
_____
_____

Cookie Design Template

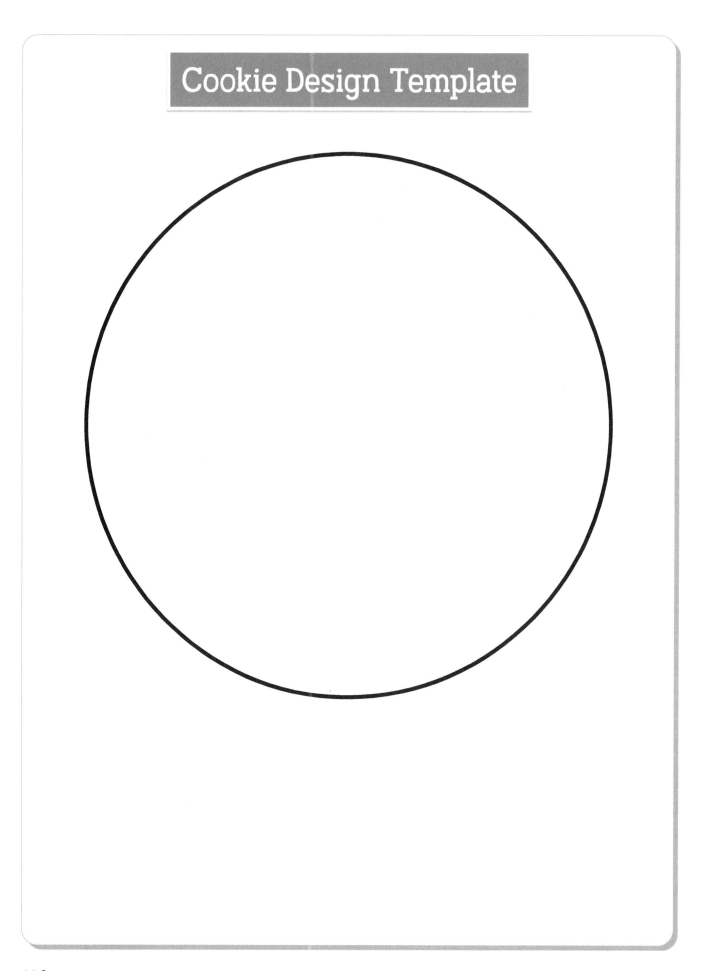

Sample Cookie Design

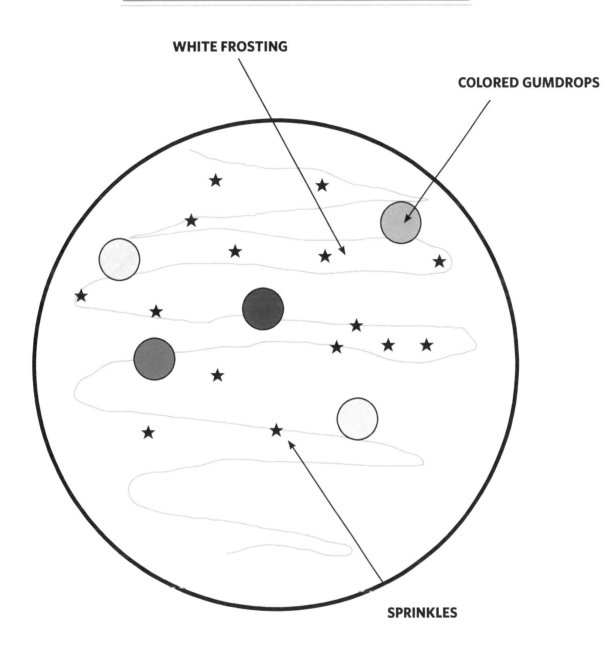

LESSON PLAN EXAMPLE: Cookie Decorating

Date: _____11/09_____

Activity: ____Cookie Design_____

Students:

_____Carrie_____	_____Gabe_____
_____Alexis_____	_____Faith_____
_____Matthew_____	_____Adam_____
_____Trevor_____	_____Elijah_____

Materials:

- ☐ Sugar cookies
- ☐ Sprinkles
- ☐ Napkins
- ☐ White frosting
- ☐ Candy
- ☐ Knives
- ☐ Colored frosting
- ☐ Paper
- ☐ Colored pencils

Expectations:

- Wash your hands first.
- Wait your turn.
- Look at the toppings on the table and consider them before you begin your design.
- Share and ask politely.
- Follow your cookie design exactly.
- Wait until everyone is finished before you eat your cookie.
- Have fun!

Steps to Complete:

1. Look at the materials on the table.
2. Draw how you want your cookie to be decorated on the Cookie Design Template.
3. Give your drawing to the instructor.
4. Wash your hands.
5. Ask for a cookie.
6. Place your cookie on the napkin.

7. Decorate your cookie to look like the picture in front of you.
8. Wait until everyone is finished.
9. Present your cookie to the group and compare how your cookie looks to the drawing.
10. Eat.

Successes:

- All students voiced frustration when they did not get their design, but most students were flexible and attempted the decoration.
- Adam noticed there were no labels on his paper, so he asked, "Who did this?"
- There was a lot of laughter.

Challenges:

- Alexis put her head down and refused to decorate her cookie when she did not get her design.
- Students did not collaborate. They just talked to themselves about it being hard.

Next Time:

- Make a step/expectation to consult with the original designer regarding how to make the cookie match the design.

STUDENT REFLECTION: Cookie Decorating

Date: _____

Activity: _____

Who was here today?

_____   _____

_____   _____

_____   _____

What did you do today?

Today we _____

_____

_____

_____

How did it make you feel?

☐ Satisfied	☐ Frustrated	☐ Bored	☐ _____
☐ Confident	☐ Irritated	☐ Sad	☐ _____
☐ Happy	☐ Anxious	☐ Shy	☐ _____

What did you do well today?

Today I was able to _____

_____

_____

_____

What was the hardest part of the activity?

The hardest part of the activity today was _____

_____

_____

_____

How did you know you were becoming frustrated?

I knew I was becoming frustrated when _____

_____

because _____

_____

_____

What can you do in class when something unexpected happens?

When something unexpected happens, I can _____

_____

_____

_____

What can you do in class when you are not sure how to do something?

In class, I can _____

_____

_____

_____

What will you do differently next time?

Next time, I will _____

_____

_____

What activity in class does this remind you of?

This activity is like _____

_____

_____

_____

Case Example: COOKIE DECORATING

One year, I presented this activity to a large group of sixth graders with Christie Bowers. The group was composed of several students on the autism spectrum and several others with expressive language disorders. One student, Marcus, was very vocal throughout the activity, often interrupting others, impulsively jumping ahead in the directions, and grabbing the candy on the table to try to taste it. When the students were told they were going to decorate cookies and eat them, he calmed down a little and listened to the directions. After I showed the students my draft of a cookie design, Marcus yelled out, "I know what I am going to draw! Toothless!" For those of you who are unfamiliar, Toothless is a black Night Fury dragon from the movie How to Train Your Dragon®. Christie and I asked Marcus if he thought that was a reasonable design and directed him to look at all the ingredients on the table, as we did not have any black frosting and the 3-inch cookies did not leave much room for detail. Marcus was adamant that it was reasonable, and he continued with a very detailed drawing of Toothless.

We gave all the students about eight minutes to create the draft design for their cookie and asked them to turn them in to us. We then posted the next section of expectations and directions. Several students protested because they were excited to decorate a cookie with their own design, and Marcus refused to decorate his cookie with a different design altogether. He then looked for the student who had his cookie design and peered over her shoulder, attempting to correct her. Because we were co-teaching the activity, I was able to take Marcus out of the room while Christie worked with the group to come up with a plan for who would eat which cookie; the students ultimately decided to switch cookies and eat the one they designed. I reflected to Marcus that his behaviors were disrupting the group and gave him a minute to argue his point. He was eventually able to be redirected to the expectations, reenter the group, and begin decorating his cookie.

As the students moved forward decorating their cookies, they asked each other for the icing, candy, and sprinkles—but not once did they ask who designed their cookie. In turn, we frequently heard kids say, "What is this?" or "I have no idea what this means," or "This is impossible." However, rather than ask for clarification, they just kept going, doing their best without any additional information.

When it came time to compare the cookies to the initial drawing, Christie and I asked the students to identify themselves as the designer and to judge whether the cookie turned out like they intended. Although a few came close, in general, most kids had a very hard time following the directions on the draft someone else made. One student started by saying, "I wanted red gumdrops and blue sprinkles, not purple gumdrops, but it looks close." Most students laughed a lot at themselves and were very kind to one another, despite feeling disappointed or frustrated. When it came time to compare Marcus's Toothless design to the original drawing, the girl who designed it put her head down and held up his picture. Although her cookie had a huge blue blob in the middle,

Marcus shouted out, "That looks exactly like it!" She picked her head up and smiled. It looked nothing like it ☺.

While students explained their cookie, Christie and I were able to insert questions such as "How could you have made sure the person intended red gumdrops?" or "If you didn't understand the design, what could you have done differently?" Eventually, students indicated that they could have asked the person who designed it for clarification. We were able to have a great discussion about what it looks like in the classroom when students are not sure of what they are supposed to do and what things they can do to get clarification before moving forward. We then attempted the cookie decorating activity again two months later, and two big changes happened. First, all the students created a very simple design for their draft, with clearly labeled ingredients down to the placement and color. Second, when they received the draft they needed to follow, they all held it over their head and simultaneously shouted, "Who drew this?"

Decorate a Door

SUMMARY

This activity takes the longest amount of time to complete, up to six sessions depending on how efficiently the group works together. This activity provides students an opportunity to set a goal and work together to accomplish the goal. Students will be required to interact with adults and present their ideas in front of others.

OBJECTIVE/GOALS

- Students will negotiate and collaborate with others to complete a task.
- Students will preplan and follow a sequence of steps to complete a long-term project.
- Students will consider another person's perspective.

SKILLS SUPPORTED

- Collaboration
- Cooperation
- Expressive Language
- Emotion Regulation
- Flexibility
- Frustration Tolerance/Perseverance
- Impulsivity
- Initiation
- Life Skills
- Locus of Control
- Organization
- Planning
- Problem Solving
- Recognizing Nonverbal Cues
- Self-Advocacy
- Self-Regulation
- Sequencing
- Shared Attention
- Taking Turns
- Theory of Mind

NUMBER OF STUDENTS

- 1–5

MATERIALS

- 8.5" × 11" paper
- Pencils
- Colored pencils or markers
- Large butcher paper
- Masking tape
- Scissors
- Notecards

PREPARATION

__ Gain permission from your administrator and classroom teacher to place something on a door.

__ Set up a time to meet with the principal so students can present their idea and request permission (Session 4).

__ Know where to get materials in the building.

INTRODUCTION

Students will decorate a door in the building that they create together. They will have to decide which door they want to decorate, get permission from the principal, come up with a design, work together, and figure out how to hang it. Share with students that this is a project that will take several weeks and that it is broken down into steps. They will be required to create a small rough draft and use it as a template to create their final product. The final product will include ideas from each student and will be hung where people can see it in the school.

EXPECTATIONS

Before you begin, review the expectations for the group and emphasize any behaviors you want to see during the session:

- Brainstorm ideas together.
- Get permission.
- Follow the steps.
- Create a rough draft.
- Share materials.
- The design must include at least two ideas from each person.
- Use the rough draft to guide the final (e.g., they should be similar).
- Think of what other people like.
- _____
- _____

STEPS

This activity is broken into six sessions, although it can take more time depending on how productive each session is. Be flexible and make adjustments based on what students are able to accomplish in one session. Everything can be rolled over into the next session.

Session 1

1. Let students know that they are going to work toward decorating a door in the school building.

2. Ask each student which door they would like to decorate and to write their preference down on the board. **Students will start with writing down or calling out their**

preferences and collectively deciding on *one* door. This is part of the problem solving involved in this activity.

3. Ask students how the group will come to an agreement regarding which door to decorate. If students get stuck, they may need support regarding the best way to decide (e.g., voting, pulling out of a hat, etc.). Often, the discussion regarding how to choose the door takes longer than expected. Encourage students to give reasons why they have chosen a certain door and to listen to other people's reasons for their choices as well. **This is a great opportunity for students to advocate for themselves, as well as to learn to compromise with others to meet a common goal.**

4. Once the students have agreed on which door they will decorate, pass out 8.5"× 11" pieces of paper to each student.

5. Instruct the students to decorate the piece of paper to reflect how they want to decorate the door. Encourage them to have a rationale that explains why they chose specific decorations.

6. Collect the designs and tell students that they will present their individual ideas to the group at the next session.

Session 2

1. Redistribute the designs from the previous session to the students.

2. Ask each student to present their design to the group. Encourage students to explain why they included certain aspects and how or why it would be a good idea to include their ideas on the door.

3. Once all the students have had an opportunity to present their ideas, ask each student to prioritize one or two aspects of their original design that they would like to have on the final product. Having them circle what they have chosen so they can refer to it will help.

4. Encourage students to discuss the overall theme or image they want to put together, including what they want the door to look like and why.

5. As the instructor, make sure to take notes on the board to help facilitate the discussion as the students problem solve how the final product should look.

6. Let the students know that during the next session, they will need to get permission from the principal before beginning the project. To do so, they will need to create a small rough draft to show the principal.

7. Take a picture of any notes that were taken during the session so you can have these ready next time.

8. Let the principal know that students will be approaching them to schedule a time to request permission to decorate a door.

Session 3

1. Refer the students to the agreed-on ideas for the door design.

2. Pull out a blank 8.5"× 11" piece of paper and ask each student to add two specific ideas to the piece of paper. **This can be a difficult part of the activity because one student might take up too much space, or students may disagree on what needs to be on the final door.** You may have to start over several times to create the draft together. The final draft should include at least two aspects of each student's original drawing.

3. Ask the students to look at how the draft looks and whether they need to add more designs or decorations to the draft.

4. Ask the students how they plan to get permission to decorate the door. As the instructor, be sure that you have talked with your building principal beforehand so you know what questions they will ask the students.

5. Let students know that they will be preparing a proposal to present to the principal during the following session.

6. Decide as a group how best to set up a meeting with the principal. Students will likely need to make an appointment either through an assistant or through the principal themself. Meeting requests can be done via email or through an in-person request.

7. At the end of the session, have the students set up the appointment with the principal. The appointment should be scheduled to occur at the end of the next session or sometime during that week. Require the students to schedule a specific time to meet with the principal rather than walking in. This provides an opportunity for students to learn how to make an appointment and how to have a brief conversation advocating for what they need.

Session 4

1. The students now know that they have an upcoming appointment with the principal, either at the end of this session or sometime this week.

2. Students need to prepare a brief presentation for this meeting that explains (a) what they would like to do, (b) where they would like to hang the door decoration, and (c) the materials they need to use. Students will bring their small rough draft to the meeting as an example.

3. Help the students create a note card with talking points so they can stay on topic when they present their proposal.

4. Assign each student at least one talking point to present to the principal.

5. Practice how they will talk with the principal before they get to their office. Rehearse potential questions so they are not caught off-guard.

6. Have the students present their proposal to the principal at the scheduled time.

Session 5

1. Present the students with a large piece of butcher paper for the final design. For older students, you can incorporate a task that requires them to collect the materials from somewhere else in the building (e.g., the art room). You can decide whether to have the materials ready beforehand or to have students collect the materials. If they need to collect the materials, it should be done prior to the start of the session.

2. Discuss with students how they will transfer their small-rough-draft ideas onto the larger piece of paper. Provide them with some time to think before they begin drawing on the final project paper.

3. Allow each student to add their own ideas to the design. You may need to encourage the use of pencils before students color in their designs with marker.

4. Have students continue to work toward completing the final design on the butcher paper. The final product will not likely be completed during the session.

Session 6

1. Finalize the decorated butcher paper.
2. Take the decorated butcher paper and masking tape to the door to be decorated.
3. Have the students hang their final project on the door, making sure not to block windows or door handles.
4. Congratulate students and reflect on how the project went, including how hard they worked for an extended time to accomplish a goal.

CHALLENGES TO INCORPORATE

− Do not premeasure the door.

− Do not have certain color markers.

+ Contribute a ridiculous idea.

+ Interrupt.

+ Say no to some ideas.

+ Assign a leadership role to a different student each session.

DIFFERENTIATION FOR AGE OR SKILL LEVEL

- **Beginner:** Although elementary-aged students can still do this project, they require a lot more support and specific direction. You will need to guide most of the steps and be explicit about what they are doing for each session. Break this activity down into three sessions with materials already available and concrete steps for completion. Young students get excited about this activity.

- **Intermediate:** Provide a rough outline of the overall steps and encourage students to fill in the details before beginning. Reflect on how their plan will work and ask guiding questions to fill in any gaps. Facilitate problem solving and provide emotion regulation prompts to support students' success. I often present this activity in the middle of the year, after students have gotten to know each other and have become part of a team with their teachers.

- **Advanced:** Rather than decorate a door, the group can consult with student-led organizations and create a poster for an activity (e.g., football game, dance, concert, etc.). I typically incorporate the activity during homecoming or prom season so they can contribute to school spirit weeks when all the other students are doing similar projects. This facilitates active participation in the high school community and interaction with other students. As the instructor, you can provide a rough outline regarding the steps and timeline. Ask guiding questions to move the group along but do not problem solve for them.

REFLECTION

A brief reflection is encouraged after each session, which can focus on any of the following points: (1) cooperation and compromise, (2) time management, and (3) how to make an appointment and be prepared.

FOLLOW-UP

Reflecting on this activity is the best form of follow-up. You can then support students in organizing for other long-term projects and follow similar steps to break the project down into steps and goals for completion. The following activities require similar skills:

- Build a Vehicle
- Cookie Decorating
- Build a Bridge
- Teacher Appreciation Cards

GENERALIZATION TO THE CLASSROOM

This activity replicates any group or long-term project that requires several steps. For younger students, it is more about working together, compromising, and making something for someone else. For older students, it provides an opportunity to practice organization, planning, time management, and following through on a long-term project.

INSTRUCTOR NOTES AND THOUGHTS

_____

_____

_____

_____

LESSON PLAN EXAMPLE: Decorate a Door

Date: _____04/25_____

Activity: _____Decorate a Door (Session 4)_____

Students:

_____Sasha_____   _____Kyle_____

_____Rachel_____   _____

_____Tony_____   _____

Materials:

☐ Notecards   ☐ Pencils

Expectations:
- Get permission.
- Listen.
- Be polite.

Steps to Complete:

1. Review door decoration draft.
2. Decide who will present each piece to the principal.
3. Prepare a short notecard to ask the principal for permission.
4. Outline the proposal, which should cover the following:
    a. What we are asking to do
    b. Where we want to hang it
    c. What materials we need
    d. When we plan on doing it
5. Decide who will present which parts of the proposal.
6. Create a note card for yourself to stay on topic.
7. Practice presenting to the group first.
8. Present the proposal to the principal.
9. Good luck!

Successes:
- Students were nervous about the meeting but got through it and stayed on topic.
- They were very excited that they made the appointment and got permission.

Challenges:
- Kyle wanted to present the whole idea and had a hard time compromising.

Next Time:
- Gather materials to create the door design.
- Begin creating the final draft on butcher paper, reminding students that it is a collaboration.

STUDENT REFLECTION: Decorate a Door

Date: _____

Activity: _____

Who was here today?

_____   _____
_____   _____
_____   _____

What did you do today?

Today we _____

_____

_____

_____

How did it make you feel?

☐ Satisfied	☐ Frustrated	☐ Bored	☐ _____
☐ Confident	☐ Irritated	☐ Sad	☐ _____
☐ Happy	☐ Anxious	☐ Shy	☐ _____

What did you do well today?

Today I was able to _____

_____

_____

_____

What was the hardest part of the activity?

The hardest part of the activity today was _____

_____

_____

_____

What are you most proud of?

I am proud that we _____

_____

_____

_____

When is it a good idea to get permission before you start a task?

I need to get permission before I _____

_____

because _____

What is it like to not get your own way when you have an idea?

When I do not get my way, I feel _____

_____

_____

_____

When things become hard, what helps you get through it?

When things are hard for me, I _____

_____

_____

_____

DECORATE A DOOR

Although I have completed this activity with students at various stages of development, this particular case example highlights my experience with a group of four elementary school students whose age and skill level made the activity take longer than expected. They all had difficulty staying on task and completing their work on time, and they were very easily distracted. For example, the entirety of the first session was spent on deciding which teacher should get their door decorated, as opposed to also having students design drafts of what they would like the door to look like. Because the students could not come to a decision, I had to create a template form so that they could rank their first, second, and third choices. Once students wrote down their preferences, I had them present their choices in front of the group, including their rationale for each choice. I began writing names on the whiteboard so we could keep track and eventually vote, and each time a teacher was nominated more than once, I put an additional checkmark next to their name on the board.

After all four students presented their cases, we had a total of nine names on the board, including seven teachers, the principal, and a paraprofessional. I then asked the students how we should decide on which door to decorate. One student shot his hand up and said, "We should vote!" I redirected him to the board and asked, "Haven't we kind of already voted?" All the group members looked toward the board and noticed that the principal had three checkmarks next to her name, and the group agreed to decorate the principal's door.

The second, third, and fourth sessions were spent creating drafts of what each individual student wanted the decorated door to look like and attempting to incorporate their ideas into a single draft. Each of the individual drafts highlighted what the students' self-interests were. One student made an entire draft of Pokémon® images, another student created an amazing Minecraft® poster, the third student had an emphasis on Iron Man® and the Avengers®, and the fourth student drew the school mascot and a bunch of stick figures. After I collected all the individual designs, I shared with the students that they had to choose two specific details from their individual draft to add to the group design. This, too, took longer than I expected because the students had a very difficult time only choosing two. They spent a significant amount of time arguing or rationalizing why each design was important and why they needed to add more than two. In an attempt to problem solve through this difficulty, we spent a lot of time talking about why we were decorating a door, who it was for, and what the most reasonable design should include given that we were putting it on the principal's door.

Eventually, I took the time to allow the students to see what would happen if they attempted to add more than two designs each. We started passing the final draft around to each student, and I told students that they could add two images each time the draft was in front of them. The students quickly saw that after each of them added two images, little room was left for anything else. At one point during the fourth session, I was not sure we would ever get the final door decoration completed, but once we agreed on a final draft, the rest quickly fell into place. Given how long the activity had already taken, I did not require the students to get permission from the principal; I took care of that for them. On the seventh week, the students were beyond proud to present their hodgepodge of a door decoration to the principal. It included the principal's name written in rainbow colors, a few streamers, and images of the school mascot, Pokémon, Iron Man, and Minecraft.

When I first began this activity, I went into it with the idea that I would help the students practice taking turns and collaborating with their peers while keeping a goal in mind to stay on topic and complete a task. Once we got started, I realized that I needed to spend more time helping them develop task sheets and other ways to recognize when they were getting off task, and the activity highlighted to me what their needs looked like in the classroom. By the end of this activity, I was able to create small accommodation sheets that the teachers could use in the classroom to help redirect their behavior. I then followed up with teachers to talk about some of the challenges they experienced and how I could better support the students in their classrooms. Keeping their IEP goals in mind, along with what teachers wanted to prioritize in the classroom, I made adjustments during subsequent group sessions to practice utilizing some of the tools we created so students could stay on task in the classroom.

Peanut Butter & Jelly

SUMMARY

This really fun activity is an excellent platform to practice effective communication. Students will be required to give directions to someone regarding how to make a peanut butter and jelly sandwich by only using their words. The activity can become silly, and students laugh a lot, but they are ultimately tasked with speaking clearly and with purpose to help a listener understand what they want to get done. This activity allows students to see how language can be extremely helpful or get in the way when communicating with others.

OBJECTIVE/GOALS

- Students will communicate clearly to get their needs met.
- Students will adjust their language to meet the listener's needs.
- Students will manage their emotions when they become frustrated.

SKILLS SUPPORTED

- Cooperation
- Emotion Regulation
- Expressive Language
- Flexibility
- Following Directions
- Frustration Tolerance/Perseverance
- Impulsivity
- Initiation
- Life Skills
- Listening
- Locus of Control
- Planning
- Problem Solving
- Recognizing Nonverbal Cues
- Self-Regulation
- Sequencing
- Shared Attention
- Theory of Mind

NUMBER OF STUDENTS

- 1–6

MATERIALS

- Loaf of bread
- Peanut butter
- Jelly
- Knives
- Napkins

PREPARATION

___ Check for allergies (the activity is to make a sandwich—you can use any ingredients).

___ Purchase the food items.

___ Schedule another adult or a general education student to participate with you to model the activity the first time.

___ Prepare the guest by telling them what to expect and how to model the activity appropriately.

INTRODUCTION

Students will be making sandwiches together today. They will be paired in groups of two, and one person will make a sandwich while the other person gives directions regarding how to make the sandwich. The person giving directions is not allowed to touch anything. To make a sandwich successfully, the student giving directions will need to watch what the listener/sandwich maker is doing and adjust their directions if the listener makes a mistake. As the instructor, model how to do the activity first, and encourage students to have fun with the activity.

EXPECTATIONS

Before you begin, review the expectations for the group and emphasize any behaviors you want to see during the session:

- Wash your hands first.
- Think about what you want to say before you tell your partner to do something.
- Be kind.
- Be patient.
- Have fun!
- _____
- _____

STEPS

1. Require students to wash their hands.
2. Place all materials in the center of the table.
3. Pair students together in groups of two.
4. With the help of another adult, model how to direct someone to make a peanut butter and jelly sandwich. **The listener in this activity needs to follow directions *exactly* as they are told and follow instructions *very literally*.** For example, if someone says, "Get out a piece of bread" without instructing you to open the bag first, try to get the bread out through the middle of the bag or by tearing the bag. If someone says, "Put peanut butter on the bread," without instructing you to open the jar or put peanut butter on a knife, place the jar of peanut butter on top of the piece of bread. (I have had my hand in peanut butter when doing this activity because the student did not instruct me to put a knife in the peanut butter ☺). Most students will find this activity funny and work through frustrations.

5. Decide whether students can work independently in their respective pairs or if the group as a whole needs to watch each pair attempt the sandwich. **If you decide to have pairs go one at a time, it provides more modeling opportunities so the next pair of students can make adjustments before jumping right in.**

6. Instruct students to begin the activity and complete a sandwich. As students begin to make their sandwiches, be sure to encourage students to listen and follow directions exactly as they are told. Often, students will fill in gaps in instruction and/or do what they think they should do rather than listen first. Students will also want to be the listener and the instructor, so if you do not have time for both, you can repeat the activity again during the next session.

7. Eat sandwiches if you want to.

8. Reflect on the session, and discuss how communication can be improved as a listener and as a communicator.

CHALLENGES TO INCORPORATE

+ Be *very* literal (e.g., do not fill in gaps of instruction).

+ Do not listen very well and/or appear distracted.

+ Get frustrated or mad.

DIFFERENTIATION FOR AGE OR SKILL LEVEL

- **Beginner:** This activity will be more successful in a small group of one or two students, with the instructor always being the listener/sandwich maker. As students provide directions, ask clarifying questions and require them to restate the direction clearly and correctly before moving on to the next step. Younger students will need more support with sequencing how to make the sandwich, and you may need to post the steps in order so they can refer to them.

- **Intermediate:** Have the group watch each pair work together so they have opportunities to learn from each other. This activity is excellent for middle school students, and it provides an opportunity for you to observe how students communicate.

- **Advanced:** Require that students be very explicit in their instruction, down to the small details (e.g., how to twist the lid off the jar or remove the twist tie from the bread bag).

REFLECTION

This is a fun way for students to *see* how they communicate their intent. Reflection can focus on how individuals can adjust their language to help the listener/sandwich maker better understand their directions. Students can also discuss how they know if someone does not understand what they are saying (e.g., recognizing nonverbal cues).

FOLLOW-UP

Students can bring in their favorite game and teach the group how to play. They might need support outlining the directions for the game and may require prompts to check for the group's understanding before moving forward. Other activities that require similar skills include the following:

- Build a Vehicle
- Back-to-Back Drawing
- Stress Ball
- Scavenger Hunt

GENERALIZATION TO THE CLASSROOM

This activity highlights the importance of listening to directions in the classroom before beginning an activity. It also provides students with an opportunity to see how they utilize expressive language to clearly communicate with others and get their needs met, as well as to recognize nonverbal cues indicating whether others understand them. It helps them understand how breakdowns in communication lead to conflict and frustration.

INSTRUCTOR NOTES AND THOUGHTS

LESSON PLAN EXAMPLE: Peanut Butter & Jelly

Date: _____08/13_____

Activity: ___Peanut Butter & Jelly___

Students:

_____Tiffany_____	_____Liam_____
_____William_____	_____
_____Ivan_____	_____

Materials:

- ☐ Loaf of bread
- ☐ Peanut butter
- ☐ Jelly
- ☐ Knives
- ☐ Napkins

Expectations:

- Wash your hands first.
- Think about what you want to say before you tell your partner to do something.
- Be kind.
- Be patient.
- Have fun!

Steps to Complete:

1. Wash your hands first.
2. Watch the example for how to make a peanut butter and jelly sandwich.
3. Sit with your partner and decide who will be the instructor and who will make a sandwich.
4. Follow the directions *exactly* how you are told.
5. Wait until everyone is finished.
6. Eat your sandwich if you want to.

Successes:

- William started using gestures to help Ivan better understand.
- Tiffany got frustrated and asked Liam for help in opening the jelly jar.

Challenges:
- William needed more support with directional language.

Next Time:
- Post descriptive phrases on the board that students can refer to when they get stuck, such as the following:
    - Place on top
    - Turn to the right
    - Hold down with one hand
    - Using your left hand
    - Using your right hand
    - Set to the left

STUDENT REFLECTION: Peanut Butter & Jelly

Date: _____

Activity: _____

Who was here today?

_____   _____
_____   _____
_____   _____

What did you do today?

Today we _____
_____
_____
_____

How did it make you feel?

☐ Satisfied   ☐ Frustrated   ☐ Bored   ☐ _____
☐ Confident   ☐ Irritated   ☐ Sad   ☐ _____
☐ Happy   ☐ Anxious   ☐ Shy   ☐ _____

What did you do well today?

Today I was able to _____
_____
_____
_____

What was the hardest part of the activity?

The hardest part of the activity today was _____
_____
_____
_____

What happens in class if you assume what comes next in an activity without listening to directions first?

In class, _____

_____

_____

_____

How can you tell if someone understands what you are talking about?

I can tell someone understands me by _____

_____

_____

_____

What will you do differently next time?

Next time, I will _____

_____

_____

_____

PEANUT BUTTER & JELLY

One year, I presented this activity to a small group of three students with the help of Christie Bowers and Max, a school psychology intern I was supervising. I was paired with a student who struggled with significant anxiety, and Christie and Max were paired with students diagnosed with autism spectrum disorder. Christie and her student, David, were the first pair to start, with David giving instructions and Christie serving as the sandwich maker. Christie has always been an ideal person to model this activity because she follows directions very literally and with a straight face. For example, when David instructed her to open the bag and pull out a piece of bread, Christie ripped open the bag right in the middle of the package. David said, "Ugh, not like that!" He appeared to get stuck with his directions but eventually pointed his finger and said, "In this side, right here. Very gently and only take out two pieces."

As Christie continued to be a difficult listener, David started pausing before giving his next direction because he knew she was just going to mess up. He also started using gestures to describe what to do, which we had never seen him do before. He started being much more thoughtful and purposeful with his instructions and ended up with a sandwich that he could eat. At one point, however, David directed her to, "Pick up the knife, hold it, and get a handful of peanut butter." Everyone in the room started laughing in anticipation of what was to come next. David became nervous and looked around the table with uncertainty as Christie's hand hovered over the peanut butter jar. I directed him to watch what she was doing, and he said, "No! Not like that! Use your knife!" and started laughing too.

As the other pairs in the group watched David's progress, they started leaning over and whispering what they thought he should say next. They had already begun coming up with plans to make their own process go more smoothly. Therefore, when it was Max and Joe's turn to go, Joe began by giving directions to Max cautiously, although he still became very irritated when Max followed directions too literally. For example, when Joe instructed Max to grab the peanut butter knife, Max grabbed it by the side that had peanut butter all over it. Joe was very bothered, but he took a deep breath and instructed Max to put the knife down and pick it up on the handle side. As Max continued being a difficult listener, Joe became increasingly irritated; his tone changed, and he became very short with Max. However, he continued to give directions and remained composed, which was impressive because Joe typically yelled and called us names when he got frustrated. By the time Max finished his sandwich, his hands were covered with peanut butter and Joe was ready to watch someone else, but he had completed the activity without losing his temper.

When it was my turn to take directions from Aaron, he had already watched the two boys go before him and made several adjustments with his directions. The first few steps went smoothly, but Aaron had a limited vocabulary and often tried to demonstrate what I should do by using hand signals. He patiently encouraged me to try using clockwise and counterclockwise turns to open the peanut butter jar, and once I got it open, he used his pointer finger to demonstrate a scooping motion. I copied him with my index finger and raised my eyebrows as if to ask, "Are you sure?" He said yes, so I put my finger in the peanut butter and swiped some out. He slammed his head in his hand, and David said, "Great, now we can't use that peanut butter!"

In the end, each student successfully instructed the adults how to make a peanut butter and jelly sandwich. Seeing how patient they were while trying to come up with the best way to instruct us to complete very small, simple steps was amazing. The activity was also appealing to them because seeing adults not having a clue what to do was silly. We had a great discussion about how it is problematic to assume that others know what we are thinking or trying to convey. We talked about how important it is to look for cues when talking to other people to see if they understand us or if we need to add more information.

Back-to-Back Drawing

SUMMARY

This is another communication activity where students are required to convey their thoughts clearly and succinctly for a listener to complete a task. Students will give directions to a partner regarding how to reproduce a drawing that the partner cannot see. This activity is challenging and fun, and it requires students to think before they speak and utilize language intentionally.

OBJECTIVE/GOALS

- Students will plan and organize their thoughts to communicate clearly.
- Students will adjust their language to meet the listener's needs.
- Students will manage their emotions when they become frustrated.

SKILLS SUPPORTED

- Cooperation
- Emotion Regulation
- Expressive Language
- Flexibility
- Following Directions
- Frustration Tolerance/Perseverance
- Impulsivity
- Initiation
- Listening
- Locus of Control
- Organization
- Planning
- Problem Solving
- Self-Regulation
- Sequencing
- Shared Attention
- Taking Turns
- Theory of Mind

NUMBER OF STUDENTS

- 1–6

MATERIALS

- 8.5" × 11" plain paper
- Colored pencils

PREPARATION

__ Have some prepared designs ready to hand out (see example designs on pages 161-163).

__ Review and post descriptive vocabulary words before beginning the activity (e.g., *left*, *right*, *vertical*, *horizontal*, *large*, *medium*, *small*).

INTRODUCTION

Students will be working in pairs and instructing each other to reproduce a drawing without looking. Students will sit back-to-back. One student in the pair will have a drawing in their hand, while the other will have a blank piece of paper and some colored pencils. The student with the picture needs to give clear directions to their partner so that the partner can reproduce the picture on the blank piece of paper. When students are finished, they will compare the two drawings.

EXPECTATIONS

Before you begin, review the expectations for the group and emphasize any behaviors you want to see during the session:

- Think about what you want to say before you tell your partner to do something.
- Use simple descriptive words so your partner can visualize what you are saying.
- Be kind.
- Be patient.
- Have fun!
- _____
- _____

STEPS

1. Model the entire process with another adult or student first.
2. Divide students into pairs.
3. Decide whether students can work independently in their respective pairs or the group as a whole needs to watch each pair attempt the drawing. **Observing their peers complete the activity helps them see what it looks like, and it provides them opportunities to adjust their own behaviors and/or give feedback to others.**
4. Post descriptive vocabulary words that students can see and refer to during the activity. **Often, students have difficulty describing the size, orientation, and shape of the designs on the paper. Having vocabulary words written down that students can reference if they become stuck helps, or you can guide some of the instruction if needed.** You will have to decide how much support students receive so they do not become overly frustrated.
5. Ask students in the pair to sit back-to-back.
6. Hand out a piece of paper with a drawing on it to one student in the dyad and a plain piece of paper and colored pencils to the other student.

7. Instruct the student with the design to begin giving directions to the listener regarding how to re-create the drawing. Let the student know that the purpose is to make an exact duplicate. **This activity highlights where students have difficulty with communication—including limited vocabulary, sequencing, and planning—and whether they are able to convey a general description of the drawing before getting into specific details.** Students may need to be encouraged to ask clarifying questions when they are drawing. Often, they will continue drawing even if they misunderstand or do not hear their partner.

8. Once the drawing is finished, compare the original design to the duplicate.

9. Reflect on the exercise, and discuss how communication can be improved as a listener and as a communicator.

CHALLENGES TO INCORPORATE

− Start with the paper in the wrong orientation.

+ Mess up when you are the listener.

+ Ask a lot of clarifying questions, as this will frustrate students who are serving as the communicator if they think they are being clear.

DIFFERENTIATION FOR AGE OR SKILL LEVEL

- **Beginner:** Make very simple designs and post descriptive vocabulary words that will support students in re-creating the design. Make designs that look like something students are familiar with (e.g., tree, house, car).
- **Intermediate:** Follow the instructions as they are.
- **Advanced:** Instruct students to make their own design, encouraging them to keep it simple. This is a true test of theory of mind because when students are designing their picture, they have to think about how difficult it will be for the other person to reproduce it.

REFLECTION

Reflection for this activity focuses on how students organize their thoughts and communicate clearly so another person can understand. Reflection can also focus on the importance of listening completely before beginning or completing a task and asking clarifying questions when you do not understand a direction.

FOLLOW-UP

Play games that require students to describe things, such as Heads Up! or Telephone. Other activities that require similar skills include the following:

- Build a Vehicle
- Peanut Butter & Jelly
- Scavenger Hunt

GENERALIZATION TO THE CLASSROOM

This activity is another that highlights the importance of listening to directions in the classroom before beginning an activity. It also provides students with opportunities to advocate for themselves when they are unsure of what they are doing.

INSTRUCTOR NOTES AND THOUGHTS

Back-to-Back Design Examples

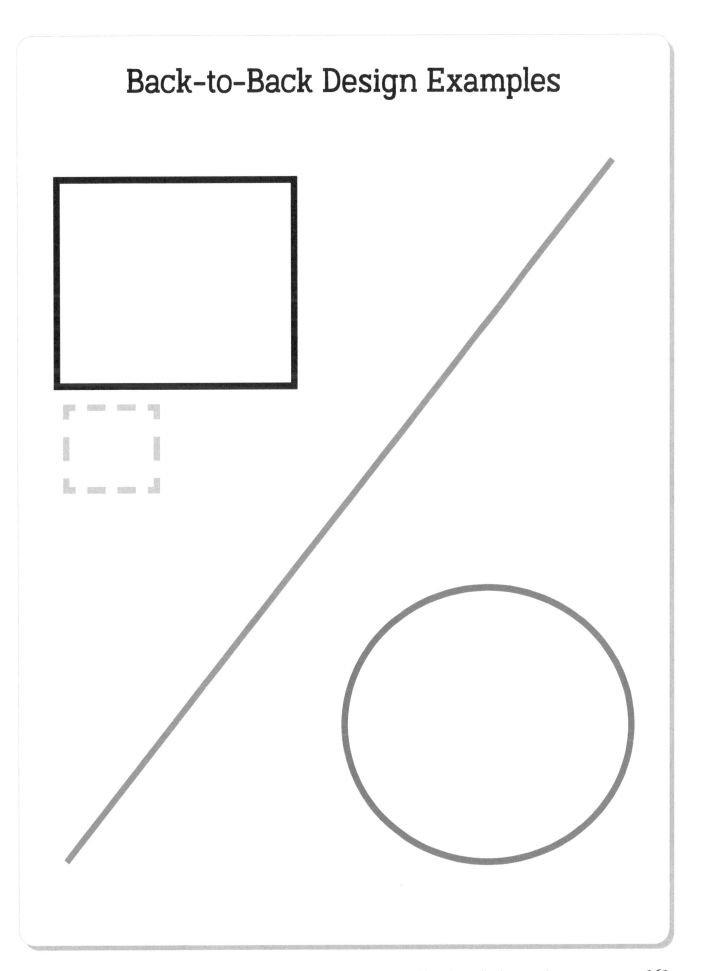

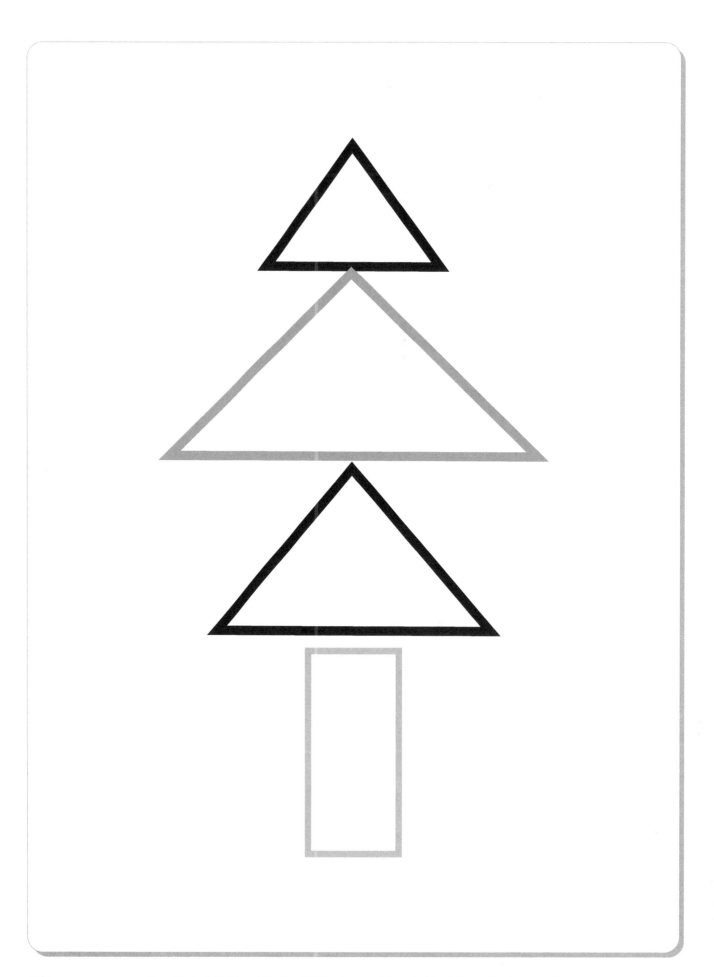

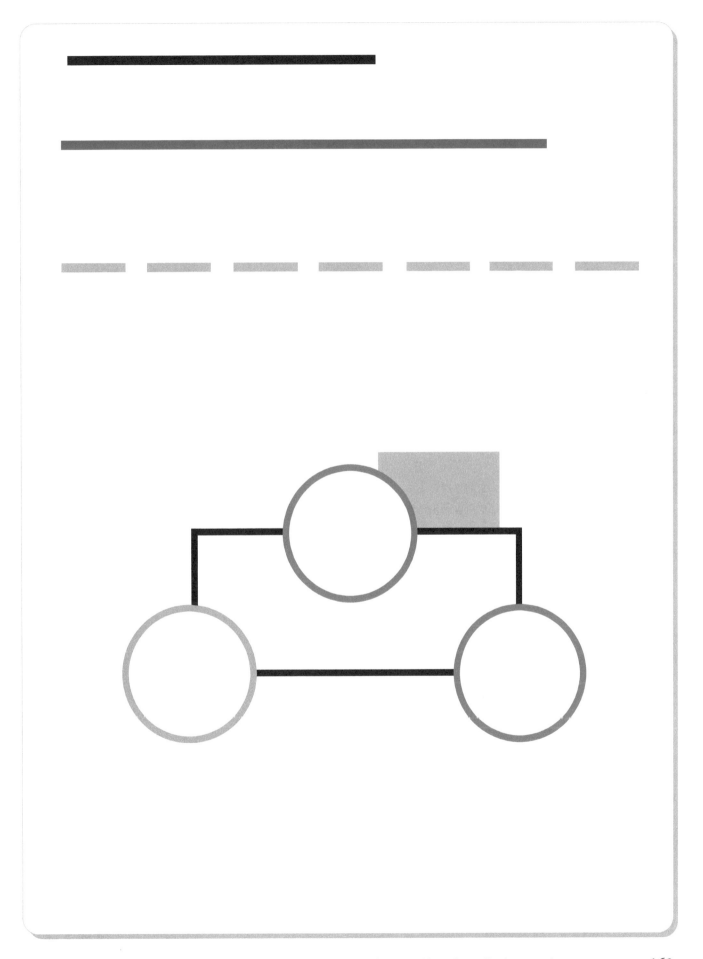

LESSON PLAN EXAMPLE:
Back-to-Back Drawing

Date: _____10/10_____

Activity: _____Back-to-Back Drawing_____

Students:

_____Parker_____	_____Sarah_____
_____Colby_____	_____
_____Zach_____	_____

Materials:

☐ 8.5" x 11" plain paper

☐ Colored pencils

Expectations:

- Think about what you want to say before you tell your partner to do something.
- Use simple descriptive words so your partner can visualize what you are saying.
- Be kind.
- Be patient.
- Have fun!

Steps to Complete:

1. Watch the instructor model the activity.
2. Sit back-to-back with your partner.
3. The person who has the design is the communicator, and the other person is the listener.
4. The communicator gives directions to the listener so they can make an exact copy of the design. (Do not show the listener the design!)
5. Compare your design to the original design.

Successes:
- Parker asked for help.
- Sarah asked to take a break from drawing to get water because she was frustrated. She then came back and tried again.

Challenges:
- This activity was hard for everyone.
- Students did not describe things in terms of size and began describing details of the picture before starting with a general description.
- No one could orient themselves on the page.

Next Time:
- Model the activity a few more times.
- Make the designs simpler.
- Outline the steps to describe the picture. For example,
    1. "Orient the paper correctly."
    2. "The picture looks like [*general description*]."
    3. "Start in the upper right corner with [*more specific description*]."

STUDENT REFLECTION: Back-to-Back Drawing

Date: _____

Activity: _____

Who was here today?

_____   _____

_____   _____

_____   _____

What did you do today?

Today we _____

_____

_____

_____

How did it make you feel?

☐ Satisfied	☐ Frustrated	☐ Bored	☐ _____
☐ Confident	☐ Irritated	☐ Sad	☐ _____
☐ Happy	☐ Anxious	☐ Shy	☐ _____

What did you do well today?

Today I was able to _____

_____

_____

_____

What was the hardest part of the activity?

The hardest part of the activity today was _____

_____

_____

_____

What can you do in class when you are not sure about what you are doing?

In class, I can _____

_____

_____

_____

What will you do differently next time?

Next time, I will _____

_____

_____

_____

BACK-TO-BACK DRAWING

I once presented this activity to a group of high school students who had difficulties with their communication skills. In particular, the members in the group often communicated using vague language, and they frequently talked about very specific areas of interest that most other people do not know much about. They struggled when it came to active listening, especially with regard to interpreting nonverbal cues and asking clarifying questions. Throughout the year, we had worked on how to recognize nonverbal cues to determine if your listener needs more information to understand you, and the group members were having a hard time demonstrating an understanding of that concept.

Similar to the Peanut Butter & Jelly activity, I paired students, and we all watched one team go at a time so we could learn from each other. I explained that the point of the activity was to clearly explain a picture so that someone behind you could re-create it by hand. I showed them a sample of a simple picture I had drawn and modeled how to describe the picture while another student drew it according to my directions. I wrote some descriptive words on the board that they could refer to if they got stuck (e.g., horizontal, vertical, short, long, large, small, medium, upper left, lower right), and I gave them about five minutes to create a drawing to describe to their partner. I encouraged them to keep it simple and easily recognizable.

Two students in the group, John and Alex, were paired together, with John serving as the communicator and Alex as the listener who was tasked with re-creating the drawing. John had drawn a picture of the Minecraft character, Steve, and a diamond sword. Although Minecraft was a particular area of interest for John, it was not necessarily something that all the group members knew about. John frequently talked about Minecraft and had a difficult time picking up on cues from others that they were either bored or did not have a clue as to what he was talking about. John began instructing Alex by saying, "Draw a big, blue rectangle. Then, draw a small rectangle on top of the big rectangle." He proceeded to instruct Alex to draw rectangles and squares attached to the big rectangle, but at no point did he say that the picture should look like the Minecraft character Steve. (For reference, Steve is a geometric-looking character whose body is composed of squares and rectangles.)

John continued giving directions to re-create the drawing, all the while assuming that Alex knew it was Minecraft. Alex continued to draw what he was instructed to but kept throwing his hands up and making faces in confusion. Although Alex happened to be a very good artist, the final result he created was a bunch of squares and rectangles, none of which looked like Steve. All the group members had a good laugh when they compared the two drawings.

When I asked John what he thought about the activity, he replied, "I don't know how he didn't figure it out!" Alex argued, "You never said it was Steve! That would have helped some." I pointed out to Alex that he often looked confused when John was talking, yet he never asked John any clarifying questions. Similarly, John never assumed that Alex may have needed more specific information to complete the drawing. The activity presented them both with a challenge that highlighted what they need to learn to do when communicating with others: (1) include additional details when explaining things to others, (2) consider the perspective of the listener, and (3) ask questions when you are confused or do not know what is being asked of you.

Plan a Party

SUMMARY

This activity is the most complex, which can take between four to six weeks to complete, depending on the age of the children, their skill level, and the amount of support you provide. Students will work together to host a party with snacks and activities to enjoy with some of their peers. This activity is great for celebrating all the hard work students have shown all year. This activity requires a lot of patience from the instructor, but it is one of the most rewarding experiences.

OBJECTIVE/GOALS

- Students will negotiate and collaborate with others to complete a task.
- Students will stay on task and regulate their emotions to complete a project with others.
- Students will consider another person's perspective.

SKILLS SUPPORTED

- Collaboration
- Cooperation
- Emotion Regulation
- Flexibility
- Following Directions
- Frustration Tolerance/Perseverance
- Impulsivity
- Initiation
- Life Skills
- Listening
- Locus of Control
- Organization
- Planning
- Problem Solving
- Recognizing Nonverbal Cues
- Self-Advocacy
- Self-Regulation
- Sequencing
- Shared Attention
- Taking Turns
- Theory of Mind

NUMBER OF STUDENTS

- 1–6

MATERIALS

- Paper
- Pencils
- Computer with internet access and a printer
- Telephone

PREPARATION

　__ Look at the calendar to have some dates and times in mind.

　__ Check with the administration to see if it will support the party with a budget and how much.

　__ Be sure you know how to order through the school or get reimbursed for purchases.

　__ Communicate with students' parents so they know what the students are planning.

　__ Plan a scheduled time with the administrator for students to present their budget.

　__ If students will be ordering food, call ahead to let them know a student will be placing an order.

　__ Decide ahead of time if you want the consequence to be not having a party if the students do not prepare it.

　__ Check for allergies.

INTRODUCTION

Students will be planning a party for the group and a few friends. Each student will invite two people, one of whom can be a teacher or a parent. This activity takes a few weeks to prepare, so students need to pick a date and come up with ideas to have a fun time. Students will make invitations and choose food and activities to have at the party.

EXPECTATIONS

Before you begin, review the expectations for the group and emphasize any behaviors you want to see during the session:

- Work together.
- Think about what other people might like.
- Compromise.
- Get permission.
- _____
- _____

STEPS

Session 1

1. Create an outline on the board that includes the following issues to consider, or use the "Party Planning Sheet" on pages 177-178:

    a. Deciding how many people to invite (and making invitations)

    b. Deciding what to have at the party (e.g., drinks, food, supplies, games). Games should include those you have already played throughout the year so students are familiar with the rules and how to play successfully.

    c. Finalizing the budget

    d. Getting permission from principal

    e. Setting the date and time

2. Pull out a calendar and decide as a group when it would be reasonable to host the party, given all the tasks that need to be completed on the board. The timeframe should be at least four weeks out. Ideally, the party will be scheduled close to or during your scheduled group session or during lunchtime or a free period. On the day of the party, you will see the students a little longer than you typically do, so you may need to get permission from their teachers ahead of time.

3. You have already shared with the group that each student will invite two people. Because that has been the instruction, ask the students to figure out how many people will be invited to the party. Do not ask them to decide who at this time. **This can cause some stress, particularly for students who have no idea who to invite or for those who want to invite too many people.** Given that some students will quickly think to invite adults in the building or their parents, requiring that they invite at least one other student is best. During the session, you can have a lot of discussion about how you know someone will be a good person to invite and how you invite someone to do something with you.

4. Ask students what types of things they would like to have at the party. Do not put limitations on anything at this time, and help them break things down into categories such as food, drinks, games, and supplies. You can use the provided party planning sheet or brainstorm ideas on the board.

5. Let students know that they will have to ask the principal permission to purchase these items and that they need to keep in mind the convenience of items as well (e.g., cooking things will be too hard).

6. Discuss the items in each column and whether it is reasonable to have each item at a small class party and why. In addition, consider any food allergies.

7. Decide together what items to include on the final supply list.

8. Encourage students to start thinking about which two people they want to invite.

Session 2

1. Pull out the party planning sheet from the previous session.

2. Ask students to estimate how much each item on the list costs and to write down their estimate next to each item. They will often underestimate the costs of things.

3. Ask students how they can know for sure how much the items cost so they can submit an accurate budget request to the principal. **Encourage students to look up information online if they cannot come up with it on their own and to pay attention the next time they go to the grocery store.**

4. Complete a budget sheet so students know how much money they will be asking for. Encourage them to consider tax and some other unexpected costs; you will need to ask for a little more money than expected.

5. Decide as a group how students will ask for budget support from the administrator.

6. Create note cards for the students with simple information that summarizes how to approach the administrator, and role-play asking permission before the students approach them. **Remember, you should have already had the party approved before students ask.** Note cards should include some of the following points:

a. "We would like to have a party on _____."

   b. "We are here to ask you for some money for the party."

   c. Present the budget and items necessary for the party.

   d. Invite the administrator ☺.

7. Let students know that they will need to decide which two people they want to invite before the next session because you will be making invitations.

Session 3

1. Ask students who they would like to invite to the party. Encourage students to choose one or two peers or one peer and one adult. **For students who have a difficult time identifying a peer they want to invite, do not force them to do so.**

2. Make a list of the people who will be invited to the party.

3. Decide how students will invite others to the party. Invitations can be sent through email, a small paper invitation, or verbally. Discuss the pros and cons of each approach.

4. Make an invitation together. Brainstorming and typing up an invitation on the computer is easiest. The invitation should include information regarding the date, time, and location of the party.

5. Print the invitations and discuss the appropriate time and place to deliver invitations to those who are being invited. If invitations are being delivered verbally, practice what students can say.

Session 4

1. Establish final preparations for the party.

2. Decide as a group how they will get the items they need for their party. As the instructor, you will typically need to purchase chips, drinks, and utensils with the money given by the school. However, students will sometimes offer to bring items in. If they offer to bring items, give them a reminder note and/or email their parents to bring in the items on a prescribed date. However, if they forget, do not rescue them. Ask them to drop the items off in your room the day before the party.

3. If the group has decided to order food (e.g., pizza), assign one student to be responsible for that task. Ask if anyone has had to order pizza before and find out how they did so. This session can be a long discussion about how to look up a phone number, ask questions about pricing, and order appropriately.

4. Practice a mock phone call for ordering pizza with each student, even if they are not assigned to do the actual ordering.

5. Delegate who will be responsible for setting up the various aspects of the party (e.g., games, drinks, seating, food table).

6. Create a map of the room and label where they decide to place things so they can be efficient when it is time to set up the party.

Note: The day before the party, bring the student who is responsible for ordering the pizza to your room and help them make the phone call for the pizza to be delivered the following day. Calling the pizza parlor before having the student call is a good idea so you can let them know that a student will be calling and that it may take a while to get through the order. A phone call from you on the front end helps the call go smoothly, and the receiver is much more patient. With the student, create a note card that contains important pieces of information, and sit with the student during the phone call.

Session 5

1. Students will be setting up the party today, so they should arrive approximately 20 to 30 minutes before the planned party time.
2. Post the map of the room with the labeled sections for where to place everything. Instruct the students to set up the room. Only provide support if students become frustrated or overwhelmed.
3. Once the room has been set up, have one more brief discussion praising them for the hard work they put into the party, and encourage them to have fun.

CHALLENGES TO INCORPORATE

– Provide less support with the brainstorming.

– Act like you do not know how to look up or find something.

+ Be adamant about including a food item (e.g., chips).

+ Disagree about drink choices.

+ Suggest something ridiculous.

DIFFERENTIATION FOR AGE OR SKILL LEVEL

- **Beginner:** Have the party planning outline ready and only ask students to brainstorm what they want to have at the party (e.g., food, games, drinks, supplies). As the instructor, you will request the budget and bring the items to the party. Parents can also donate. Students can also help create the invitations and pass them out.
- **Intermediate:** Encourage students to problem solve what needs to be incorporated in the party and give them some autonomy. When students create the party themselves, it works much better. They may need some support with the budget or in coming up with ideas for items they can bring in themselves.
- **Advanced:** Pair students and task each pair with one or two specific aspects of the party and allow them to see it through to completion. For example, if two students are in charge of food, they will be responsible for getting the opinions of the group, researching how much items cost, and ordering or purchasing the food. Encourage them to make a detailed budget and to schedule the party at an appropriate time. This activity can facilitate several life skills that the students can practice with your support.

REFLECTION

A brief reflection is encouraged after each session. This activity is typically done at the end of the school year and requires students to apply most of their learned skills throughout each session. Reflection can focus on any of the following points: (1) cooperation and compromise, (2) appropriate social interactions and activities, and (3) staying on task and considering other people's interests.

FOLLOW-UP

Reflecting on this activity is the best follow-up so students can tie their experiences with their behaviors and emotions. You can also play age-appropriate games that further support the development of social skills and add strategies to students' existing toolbox, such as Candy Land®, Twister®, Checkers, 5 Second Rule, Headbandz®, Taboo®, or Dungeons and Dragons® (for older students). Other activities that require similar skills include the following:

- Decorate a Door
- Peanut Butter & Jelly
- Scavenger Hunt

GENERALIZATION TO THE CLASSROOM

This activity imitates social interactions that students have outside of the classroom. It provides them with an opportunity to think about what they need to do to host a social gathering or party, to learn some social norms, and to practice interacting with others successfully.

INSTRUCTOR NOTES AND THOUGHTS

_____
_____
_____
_____
_____
_____

Party Planning Sheet

Date and Time: _____

Number of People: _____

Brainstorm: _____

Food	Drinks	Supplies	Games
_____	_____	_____	_____
_____	_____	_____	_____
_____	_____	_____	_____
_____	_____	_____	_____
_____	_____	_____	_____
_____	_____	_____	_____
_____	_____	_____	_____
_____	_____	_____	_____

Budget:

	Agreed List	Estimated Cost	Actual Cost
Food	_____	_____	_____
	_____	_____	_____
	_____	_____	_____
	_____	_____	_____
	_____	_____	_____
	_____	_____	_____
	_____	_____	_____
	_____	_____	_____

	Agreed List	**Estimated Cost**	**Actual Cost**
Drinks	_____	_____	_____
	_____	_____	_____
	_____	_____	_____
	_____	_____	_____
	_____	_____	_____
	_____	_____	_____
	_____	_____	_____
	_____	_____	_____

	Agreed List	**Estimated Cost**	**Actual Cost**
Supplies	_____	_____	_____
	_____	_____	_____
	_____	_____	_____
	_____	_____	_____
	_____	_____	_____
	_____	_____	_____
	_____	_____	_____
Games	_____	_____	_____
	_____	_____	_____
	_____	_____	_____
	_____	_____	_____
	_____	_____	_____
	_____	_____	_____
	_____	_____	_____
	_____	_____	_____

Total budget to ask principal = $ _____

PARTY PLANNING SHEET:

Date and Time: 05/31 at 1:00 pm

Number of people: 16

Brainstorm:

Food	Drinks	Supplies	Games
Pizza	Mountain Dew®	Napkins	Simon Says®
Chips	Root Beer	Plates	Hangman
Cupcakes	Lemonade	Forks	Candy Land
Sandwiches	Water	Cups	Sorry!
Spaghetti	Soda water	Table	Heads Up!
Pretzels	Juice	Chairs	Apples to Apples
Mac and cheese	Milk	Necklaces	UNO
M&Ms		Stickers	
Skittles			
Nuts			
Fruit			

Budget:

	Agreed List	Estimated Cost	Actual Cost
Food	Starburst®	$0.50	$2.69
	4 bags of chips	$10.00	$19.16
	24 mini cupcakes	$3.00	$4.99
	Almonds	$5.00	$6.49
	Pizza x 4	$25.00	$23.96

	Agreed List	**Estimated Cost**	**Actual Cost**
Drinks	Lemonade x 2	$2.00	$7.98
	Water	Free	0.00
Supplies	Plates	$4.00	$6.57
	Napkins	$2.50	$1.83
	Cups	$3.00	$3.99
Games	Heads Up!	We have it	0.00
	UNO	We have it	0.00
	Hangman	Free	0.00
		Total	$77.66
		Tax (8 %)	$6.21
		Backup money	$15.00
			$98.87

Total budget to ask principal = $100.00 (easy round number)

LESSON PLAN EXAMPLE: Plan a Party

Date: _____05/03_____

Activity: _____Plan a Party (Session 1)_____

Students:

Ethan	Andrew
Lily	Max
Abby	

Materials:

- ☐ Paper
- ☐ Pencils
- ☐ Computer with internet access
- ☐ Telephone

Expectations:

- Work together.
- Think about what other people might like.
- Must invite two people.
- Compromise.
- Get permission.

Steps to Complete:

1. Check the calendar and choose a date.
2. Brainstorm food and drink ideas.
3. Brainstorm game ideas.
4. Consider costs and convenience.
5. Decide on a final supply list.
6. Consider who to invite.

Successes:

- Students were very excited to plan a party.
- Lily and Max reminded the group of all the games they liked from their small-group work and provided excellent ideas for activities.

Challenges:

- Ethan does not want to invite a student from school. I will follow up next week with how to decide on this.
- Abby argued that Cheetos® are not chips and that they cannot be included. It took ten minutes of conversation to discuss this.

Next Time:

- Finalize food and drink budget.
- Make invitations and have more conversation about how to decide who to invite.

STUDENT REFLECTION: Plan a Party

Date: _____

Activity: _____

Who was here today?

_____   _____

_____   _____

_____   _____

What did you do today?

Today we _____

_____

_____

_____

How did it make you feel?

- ☐ Satisfied
- ☐ Confident
- ☐ Happy
- ☐ Frustrated
- ☐ Irritated
- ☐ Anxious
- ☐ Bored
- ☐ Sad
- ☐ Shy
- ☐ _____
- ☐ _____
- ☐ _____

What did you do well today?

Today I was able to _____

_____

_____

_____

What was the hardest part of the activity?

The hardest part of the activity today was _____

_____

_____

_____

How do you decide who to invite to a party or social activity?

I decide to ask someone to join me when _____

_____

_____

_____

What is hard about going to a party or social event?

At a party, _____

_____

_____

_____

What types of things can you do to make social interactions more successful?

When I am with other people, I can _____

_____

_____

_____

Case Example: PLAN A PARTY

The very first time I completed this activity was the most memorable and rewarding. I had a group of five eighth-grade boys who I had worked with since they were in sixth grade. Although they each had different diagnoses, they all had difficulty interacting with others socially. One of the students in this group was Daniel, the son of the mother I described earlier in the introduction. His mother had related to me that he had not been invited to a birthday party since fourth grade, saying, "Well, after fourth grade, kids stop inviting the whole class." This really struck a chord with me because Daniel was a kind, loyal friend, but he was shy and had some unique interests. So . . . I figured the best way for him experience a party was to help him throw his own.

When I first presented the idea of putting together an end-of-the-year party to celebrate the completion of eighth grade, the boys were excited. However, when I told them that they had to plan it, they groaned—and when I told them they were required to invite at least two friends, they said, "Never mind." After some coaxing, they agreed to throw the party, but we had to negotiate the option of inviting one friend and one adult. (They had initially wanted to invite two teachers). We set a date for the party eight weeks away and began brainstorming and planning. I took notes as they talked, and I reflected to them that they thought a party should have food, games, and music. One of the things I remember most is a conversation that took an entire session about whether Cheetos are chips or if they belong in a different food group. I am still not sure.

Planning the party was actually the easy part. The boys chose foods they wanted to have, incorporated games they were familiar with, created a budget, and felt confident asking the principal for the money. The part of the activity that actually caused them the most stress was creating invitations and choosing who to invite. Each student became very anxious at the thought of approaching someone and asking if they would come to their party. We talked about how you can know if someone is a friend, as well as when and how to present someone with an invitation. I offered to go with each of them to make the invite or to call the person to my office to make it less intimidating. I admit that I was nervous for them, but by the time it came to hand out invitations, each boy had already invited three friends and one teacher; they just needed to formalize it with the invitation. Although this caused our budget to increase a little, I let that go.

When it came time to order the pizza over the phone, this was also an experience, as it took three phone calls and a little patience. However, we ended up with cheese and pepperoni for everyone. I wish I could better describe how successful the party was. One teacher commented that he had never seen one of the students so talkative and happy. Everything about the party highlighted how they could behave and manage themselves like typical eighth graders. The boys were so proud of themselves and were excellent hosts. They made sure to make everyone feel included at the party, offered them food and drinks, and thanked them for coming. Essentially, they treated others how they would want to be treated.

Over the three years I worked with these boys, I had directly taught them specific skills and presented them with a variety of scenarios and activities to test their learning—and every aspect of what they had learned came together at some point during the party. I was elated to see them feel so comfortable and proud of what they had put together. I have to admit that I needed to step out at one point so I did not become emotional in front of them; it was such an accomplishment, and I could see how happy they all were. And although I never did get Daniel a Lamborghini, I was able to present him with an opportunity to create a budget and manage it—an attempt to start the concept of money—and leave middle school with a meaningful social interaction that he initiated with a group of friends.

Appendix

Lesson Plan

Date: _____

Activity: _____

Students:

　　_____　　　　_____
　　_____　　　　_____
　　_____　　　　_____
　　_____　　　　_____

Materials:

　　_____　　　　_____
　　_____　　　　_____
　　_____　　　　_____
　　_____　　　　_____

Expectations:

　　_____　　　　_____
　　_____　　　　_____
　　_____　　　　_____
　　_____　　　　_____

Steps to Complete:

1. _____
2. _____
3. _____
4. _____
5. _____
6. _____

Successes:

_____

_____

_____

Challenges:

_____

_____

_____

Next Time:

_____

_____

_____

References

For your convenience, purchasers can download and print worksheets and handouts from www.pesi.com/makofske

American Psychiatric Association. (2013). *Diagnostic and statistical manual of mental disorders* (5th ed.). Arlington, VA: Author.

Bronson, P. O., & Merryman, A. (2009). *Nurture shock: New thinking about children.* New York, NY: Twelve.

Buron, K. D. (2007). *A 5 is against the law! Social boundaries: Straight up!* Shawnee, KS: AAPC Publishing.

Buron, K. D., & Curtis, M. (2012). *The incredible 5-point scale* (2nd ed.). Shawnee, KS: AAPC Publishing.

Dawson, P., & Guare, R. (2009). *Smart but scattered: The revolutionary "executive skills" approach to helping kids reach their potential.* New York, NY: Guilford Press.

Gladwell, M. (2008). *Outliers: The story of success.* New York, NY: Hachette Book Group.

Ginsberg, K. R., & Jablow, M. M. (2011). *Building resilience in children and teens: Giving kids roots and wings* (2nd ed.). Elk Grove Village, IL: American Academy of Pediatrics.

Gray, C. (2015). *The new social story book* (Rev. ed.). Arlington, TX: Future Horizons, Inc.

Halloran, J. (2018). *Social skills for kids: Over 75 fun games & activities for building better relationships, problem-solving & improving communication.* Eau Claire, WI: PESI Publishing & Media.

Kuypers, L. M. (2011). *Zones of regulation: A curriculum designed to foster self-regulation and emotional control.* San Jose, CA: Think Social Publishing.

McAfee, J. L. (2002). *Navigating the social world: A curriculum for individuals with Asperger's syndrome, high-functioning autism and related disorders.* Arlington, TX: Future Horizons, Inc.

Moyer, S. A. (2009). *The ECLIPSE model: Teaching self-regulation, executive function, attribution, and sensory awareness to students with Asperger syndrome, high-functioning autism, and related disorders.* Shawnee, KS: AAPC Publishing.

Myles, B. S., Trautman, M. L., & Schelvan, R. L. (2013). *The hidden curriculum for understanding unstated rules in social situations for adolescents and young adults* (2nd ed.). Shawnee, KS: AAPC Publishing.

Schab, L. M. (2008). *The anxiety workbook for teens: Activities to help you deal with anxiety and worry.* Oakland, CA: New Harbinger Publications.

Sinek, S. (2009). *Start with why: How great leaders inspire everyone to take action.* New York, NY: Penguin Books.

Touch, P. (2012). *How children succeed.* New York, NY: Houghton Mifflin Harcourt.

Trafton, J. A., Gordon, W. P., & Misra, S. (2016). *Training your brain to adopt healthful habits: Mastering the five brain challenges* (2nd ed.). Los Altos, CA: Institute for Brain Potential.